The Second Death and the Restitution of All Things

Andrew John Jukes

BIBLIOLIFE

THE SECOND DEATH

AND THE

RESTITUTION OF ALL THINGS:

WITH SOME PRELIMINARY REMARKS ON THE

NATURE AND INSPIRATION OF HOLY SCRIPTURE.

A Letter to a Friend.

BY

ANDREW JUKES.

"Wilt thou shew wonders to the dead? shall the dead arise and praise thee? Shall thy loving-kindness be declared in the grave? or thy faithfulness in destruction?"—*Psalm* lxxxviii. 10, 11.

SIXTH EDITION.

LONDON:

LONGMANS, GREEN, AND CO.

1877.

PAGE 25

PREFACE.

A THOUGHT conceived but not expressed is at best only an unborn child, not only without any influence on the world, but of whose very existence the world may be unconscious; but once brought forth it becomes part of the living working universe, to work there its appointed season, and possibly to leave its mark for good or evil on all successive time.

The thought which is now expressed in these pages has long been growing in the writer's heart. Hidden at first and unconfessed, during the last few years it has from time to time been brought forth in conversation with trusted Christian friends. But the time seems come to give it a wider circulation. Men's hearts, now perhaps more than in any former age, are everywhere moved to enquire into the nature and inspiration of Holy Scripture, and the destiny of the human race, more especially the future state of sinners, as taught in Holy Scripture. Many are perplexed, hesitating to receive as perfect and divine a revelation, which, they are told, in the name of God consigns a large proportion of those who in some

sense at least are His offspring to everlasting misery.
And while the conclusion, uttered or unuttered, in
many hearts is, either that this doctrine cannot
really be a part of Holy Scripture, or else that what
is called Holy Scripture cannot be a perfect exposition or revelation of the mind of God our Saviour,
few even of those who receive the Bible as divine
seem able to solve the difficulty, or throw much light
on those portions of the " oracles of God," which confessedly are " dark sayings" and " hard to be understood."

A friend, whose mind had been unsettled by this
subject, lately expressed to the writer of these pages
some part of his perplexity. The following letter
was the result. The writer feels the solemn respon-
sibility of dissenting on such a question from the
current creed of Christendom ; and nothing but his
most assured conviction that the popular notion of
never-ending punishment is as thorough a misunderstanding of God's Word as the doctrine of Transubstantiation, and that the one as much as the other
conduces directly to infidelity, though both equally
claim to stand on the express words of Holy Scripture, would have led him to moot a subject which
cannot even be questioned in some quarters without
provoking the charge of heresy. Truth is worth all
this, and much more. If we will not buy it at all cost,
we are not worthy of it. The writer has felt more
the force of the consideration, how far, granting its
truth, the doctrine of the Restitution of All Things

is one to be proclaimed generally. Truth spoken
before its time may be not hurtful only, but even
most unlawful. The Christian truth, that "there is
no difference between the Jew and the Greek," and
that "circumcision is nothing," would surely have
been unlawful, because untimely, in the Jewish age.
So even now there may be many eternal verities
which are beyond what St. Peter calls "the present
truth," and which may therefore "not be lawful for
a man to utter." But the fact that God Himself is
ever opening out His truth seems a sufficient reason
for making it known as far as He opens it. Is not
His opening it to His servants an intimation to them
that His will is that they should declare and publish
it ? Age after age the day arrives to utter something which till the appointed day is come has been
"a secret hid in God." The very gospel which we
all believe once jarred on many minds as a doctrine
directly opposed to and subversive of the law given
by God to Moses. The doctrine here stated, therefore, though it runs like a golden thread through
Holy Scripture, may, because as yet it has been
hidden from many of God's children, be condemned
by them as contrary to God's mind, just as Paul's
gospel, when first proclaimed, was charged with being
opposed to that old law of which it was but the fulfilment. In every age the man of faith can only
say, "We having the same spirit of faith, according
as it is written, I believed, and therefore have
I spoken; we also believe, and therefore speak."

Truth may, and indeed must, vary in form as time
goes on,—Christ Himself, the Truth, at different
stages appears differently,—for God has stooped to
this, to give us truth as we can bear it; stooped
therefore to be judged as inconsistent; because He
is Love, and waits to reveal Himself till we are prepared for the revelation. But the end will justify
all His ways; and some of His children can even
now justify Him.

The night is far spent, the day is at hand. And
as in early dawn the stars grow dim, because the day
is coming, so now the lesser lights which have been
guides in darker days are paling before the coming
Sun of Righteousness. And though those who go
up to the hill-tops and watch the east may see more
of the light than those who are buried in the valleys
or sleep with closed shutters, all who look out at the
glowing firmament may see signs of coming day.
Men must be fast asleep indeed, if they do not
perceive that a new age is even now upon us.

The writer would only add that he will be thank-
ful for any suggestions or corrections on the subject
of the following pages. Any letter addressed to him,
to the care of the Publishers, will be duly forwarded
and acknowledged.

March 25, 1867.

CONTENTS.

Contents.

Contents.

RESTITUTION OF ALL THINGS,

&c.

My Dear C——

The account you give of your perplexity,
and of the answers with which it has been met by
some around you, reminds me, (if one may refer to
it in such a connection,) of what happened some
months ago in a Sunday-school. The boys in one
of the classes were reading the chapter which records
how David, as he walked on the roof of his house,
saw Bathsheba. One of the boys, looking up through
the school-room window at the steep roofs of the
houses opposite, after a pause, said,—" But, Teacher,
how could David walk on the roof of his house?"
The teacher, on this point as ignorant as his
scholar, at once checked all enquiry by saying,
"Don't grumble at the Bible, boy." Meanwhile the
teacher of an adjoining class had overheard the
conversation. Leaning over to his fellow-teacher he
whispered, "The answer to the difficulty is, 'With
men it is impossible, but not with God, for with
God all things are possible.'" Such was the solution
of "the difficulty;" too true a sample, I fear, of the

way in which on the one hand honest doubts are often met, as though all enquiry into what is perplexing in Scripture must be criminal; and on the other, of the absurdities which are confidently put forth as true expositions of God's mind and word.

Your difficulty is, how are we, as believers in Scripture, to reconcile its prophetic declarations as to the final restitution of all things, with those other statements of the same Scripture, which are so often quoted to prove eternal punishment. Scripture, you say, affirms that God our Father is a Saviour, full of pity towards the lost, seeking their restoration; so loving that He has given for man His Only-Begotten Son, in and by whom the curse shall be overcome, and all the kindreds of the earth be blessed; and yet that some shall go away into everlasting punishment, where their worm dieth not and the fire is not quenched. How is it possible, you ask, to reconcile all this? Are not the statements directly inconsistent? And if so, must not the statements of the Bible, as of other books, be corrected by that light of reason and conscience, which is naturally or divinely implanted in every one of us?

Now I grant at once that there is a difficulty here, and further that the question how it is to be solved is one deserving our most attentive consideration. I entirely agree with you also, that " though indifference or devout timidity, calling itself submission, may set aside such enquiries as unpractical or even dangerous, though indolence under the guise of humility may refuse to look at them, and spiritual selfishness, wrapt in the mantle of its own supposed security, may forbid such investigations as presumptuous, Christ-like souls can no more be unconcerned as to what may or may not be God's mind as to the mass of humanity, than they can stand by unaffected when the destitute perish from hunger, or the dying agonize in pain." All this to me seems self-evident. But, agreeing with you in this, I cannot grant that the difficulty you urge is unanswerable, or that, even if it were, you would be wise for such a reason to reject the Scriptures. Is there any revelation which God has given free from difficulties? Are there not even difficulties as to the present facts of life which are quite inexplicable? Is it not a fact that man comes into this world a fallen creature; and yet that God who made man is just, holy, and merciful ? But how do you reconcile the facts? You think that man is not a sinner only because he does evil. You rather believe that he does evil because he is a sinner, and that, guard and train him as you will, evil will come out of him because it is already in him; that in the best there is an inability to do the good they would; that in all there is a self-will and self-love, the pregnant root of sin of every kind. And yet you say that God is good. Say that the evil came through Adam's disobedience; yet how is it just to make us suffer for a trespass committed thousands of years before we were born? That there is a difficulty here is

evident from the many attempts which have been
made to solve it. Yet you and I believe both sides
of the mystery. We believe that man by nature is
corrupt, his heart wrong from his mother's womb,
a dying sinful creature, who cannot change or save
himself, utterly hopeless but for God's redeeming
mercy; and yet that God is good, and that He does
not mock us when He declares that not He, but we,
are blameable. Why then, seeing that life is such
a mystery, and that there are contradictions in it
which seem irreconcileable, and for the true answer
to which we have often to wait, should you take the
one difficulty you urge as a sufficient reason for
hastily rejecting those Scriptures, which you have
often found to be as a light in a dark place? Rather
look again and again more carefully into them.
Then you will see, as I think I see, how these Scriptures, rightly divided, open out far more exalted and
glorious hopes for man than his own unaided imagination or understanding has ever yet dared to guess
or been able to argue out.

§ I. *The Nature of Scripture.*

But before I come to the testimony of Scripture,
let me clear my way by a few words as to its nature
and inspiration. The mystery of the Incarnate
Word, I am assured, is the key, and the only sufficient one, to the mystery of the Written Word; the
letter, that is the outward and human form, of which

answers to the flesh of Christ, and is but a part
of the mystery of the Incarnation of the Eternal
Word. The Incarnation, instead of being, as some
have said, different in principle to the other revelations of Himself which God has given us, is exactly in accordance with, and indeed the key to, all
of them, in one and all the unseen and invisible God
being manifested in or through His creatures, or in
some creature-form; and this because thus only
could God be revealed to creatures like us. Whether
in Nature, or Scripture, or Christ's flesh, the law is
one. The divine is revealed under a veil, and that
veil a creature-form.

(1) Let me express what I can on this subject,
though in these days what I have to say may lie open
to the charge of mysticism. The blessed fact, which
we confess as Christians, is that the Word of God
has been made flesh,—has come forth in human form
from human nature. Jesus of Nazareth is Son of
God; not partly man and partly God, but true man
born of a woman, yet with all the fulness of the God-
head bodily. So exactly is Holy Scripture the Word
of God; not half human and half divine, but thoroughly human, yet no less thoroughly divine, with
all treasures of wisdom and knowledge revealed yet
hidden in it. And just as He, the Incarnate Word,
was born of a woman, out of the order of nature,
without the operation of man, by the power of God's
Spirit; so exactly has the Written Word come out
of the human heart, not by the operation of the

human understanding, that is the man in us, but
by the power of the Spirit of God directly acting
upon the heart, that is, the feminine part of our
present fallen and divided human nature. It is of
course easy to say this is mere mysticism. God
manifest in the flesh is a great mystery. And the
manifestation of God's truth out of man's heart in
human form is of course the same, and no less a
mystery. And those who do not see how our nature
like our race is both male and female, may here find
some difficulty. But the fact remains the same, that
our nature is double, male and female, head and
heart, intellect and affection. And it is out of the
latter of these, that is the heart, that the letter of
Scripture has been brought forth, the human form
of the Divine Word, exactly as Christ was conceived
and born of the Virgin Mary, by the power of the
Holy Ghost, without an earthly father. In no other
way could God's Word come in human form. In no
other way could it come out of human nature. But
it has humbled itself so to come for us, out of the
heart of prophets and apostles; in its human form,
like Christ's flesh, subject to all those infirmities
and limitations which Christ's flesh was subject to—
thoroughly human as He was; yet in spirit, like
Him, thoroughly divine, and full of the unfathomed
depths of God's almighty love and wisdom.

Now just as the fact that Jesus was man, and as
such grew by degrees in wisdom and stature here,
and lived our life, which is a process of corruption,

and had our members of shame, and was made sin
for us, by no means disproves that He was also Son
of God, but is only a witness of the love which
brought Him here in human form; so the fact that
Holy Scripture is human proves nothing against its
being divine also, exactly as Christ was. I would
that those who are now dissecting Scripture, and
finding it under their hands to be, what indeed it is,
thoroughly and truly human, would but pause and
ask themselves, what they could have found in
Christ's flesh, had they tortured it as they now are
torturing the letter. Had it been possible for them
to have dissected that Body,—I must say it when I
see what men are doing now,—would they have
found, with the eye of sense at least, anything there
which was not purely human? The scourge, the
nails, the spear, the bitter cry, and death at last,
proved that that wounded form was indeed most
truly human. The Bishop of Natal has dissected
the letter of Scripture till it is to him as the flesh of
Christ would have been to a mere anatomist. It is
not to him a living thing to teach him, but a dead
thing to be dissected and criticized. He has proof
that it is human; he has proof that it has grown; he
has proof that death works in it, or at least touches
it; he has seen its shameful members; he does not
wish to lead any to despise the true teachings given
by this human form; for he says it has been the chan-
nel through which he has received much blessing; he
only wishes men to see that it is really human, which

of course it must be, seeing it came out of the heart
of man; but, consciously or unconsciously, he is
leading men, not from the letter to the spirit, which
would be well, but merely to reject and judge the
letter, not seeing how that letter, like Christ's flesh,
is incorruptible and shall be glorified. After all,
this too perhaps must be done : it was needful that
Christ should suffer and be put to death ; but woe to
him who rejects and slays the human form, in which,
for us, God's truth has been manifested. Yet for
this, too, mercy is in store, for they do it ignorantly
in unbelief.

The Bible then resembles, yet differs from, other
books, just as the flesh of Christ resembles and yet
differs from the flesh of other men. All the utter-
ances of good and true men are in their measure
aspects of the mystery of the Incarnation, being partial revelations in human form of God's eternal
Truth and Wisdom ; even as every good and true
man also in his measure is another aspect of the
same mystery, for God has said, " I will dwell and
walk in them," and so human forms and flesh and
blood are by grace God's tabernacles. But the Incarnation and Manifestation of the Divine Word in
the person of our Lord Jesus Christ was pre-eminent,
and infinitely beyond what the indwelling of the
Word is in other good men, though Christ took our
flesh and infirmities, and we may be filled with all
the fulness of God. In like manner the Incarnation and Manifestation of the Word of God in the

letter of Scripture is pre-eminent, and differs from other books exactly as the flesh of Christ differs from the flesh of other men. Instead of believing therefore, that, because Scripture is human, and has grown with men, and has marks of our weakness and shame and death upon it, therefore it must perish and see corruption, I believe it can never perish or see corruption. I see it is human; I see that it has grown; I see it can be judged and wounded. I believe too that it has in its composition exactly so much of perishableness as Christ's flesh had when He walked here with His apostles. But it is like Christ's body, the peculiar tabernacle of God's truth. And those who walk by it day and night know this, for they have seen, as all shall one day see, it transfigured.

(2) I proceed to shew that like Christ's flesh, and indeed like every other revelation which God has made of Himself, the letter of Scripture is a veil quite as much as a revelation, hiding while it reveals, and yet revealing while it hides; presenting to the eye something very different from that which is within, even as the veil of the Tabernacle, with its inwoven cherubim, hid the glory within the veil, of which nevertheless it was the witness; and that therefore, as seen by sense, it is and must be apparently inconsistent and self-contradictory. Both these points are important; for if God's revelations of Himself are veils, even while they are also manifestations; and if therefore they are and must be open

to the charge of inconsistency and contradiction,
this fact will help us to understand, not only why
Scripture is what it is, but also how to interpret its
varied truths and doctrines.

And here, that we may see how all God's revelations are alike, let us look for a moment at those
other revelations of Himself, the books of Nature
and Providence, which God has given us. Are they
not both veils as well as revelations, the first sense-
readings of which are never to be relied on ?

First, as to Nature, which has been called God's
formed word, and which beyond all question is a
revelation of God. Yet how does it reveal Him ?
Is it not also a veil, hiding quite as much as it
reveals of Him ? Is it not a fact that our sense-
readings, even of the clearest physical phenomena,
such as the rising and setting of the sun, are opposed
to the truth, and need to be corrected by a higher
faculty ? Is it not further a fact that Nature hides
almost more than it reveals of God our Saviour ?
Does it not seem even to misrepresent Him ? Does it
not seem also to contradict itself, with force against
force, heat against cold, darkness against light, death
against life, its very elements in ceaseless strife
everywhere ? On one side shewing a preserver, on
the other a destroyer: here boundless provision for
the support of life ; there death reigning. We know
that this contradiction has been so strongly felt by
some, that on the ground of it they have denied that
the world is the work of one superintending mind,

and have argued that it must be either the result of chance or the work of eternally opposing powers. Are there not here exactly the same contradictions and the same difficulties which we find in Scripture? Either therefore we must say, Nature is an inconsistent and lying book, and therefore we will not believe the testimony either of its barren rocks or smiling cornfields; or else we must confess some veil or riddle here. It is precisely the same riddle which we find in every other revelation.

For the book of Providence, which I may call God's wrought word, has the very same peculiarity. Providence surely is a revelation of God; and yet is it not, like Nature, a veil quite as much as a revelation? Look not only at those things which David speaks of, that God's servants suffer, while the wicked are in great prosperity and not plagued like other men; but look at born cripples and idiots, the deaf and dumb and blind, who, as far as we know, cannot be suffering for their own sake;—look at the fact that in one instance crime is punished, in another unpunished, here. Is not this inconsistent? Where is the justice of it; and where, as judged by sense, is the love of sending souls into the world whose life throughout is one of suffering? Certainly here is a text in God's providential book of rule, (which I may say answers to the books of Kings, or Rule, in Scripture,) quite as hard as any of those texts in the book of Kings, which some would cut out of Scripture, as presenting us with false and unworthy views

of Him. But can these critics blot the selfsame
text out of God's book of rule in Providence?
There it stands, just as it stands in the book of
Nature also. Shall we therefore say that the revelation of God in Providence is an inconsistent one?
No—the fact is, it is a veil as well as a revelation,
and all its apparent inconsistencies and contradictions can be cleared up, if not to sense, yet to faith,
in the light of God's sanctuary.[1]

Even so it is with those two other revelations,
which, much as they have been gainsaid, the Church
has received and yet believes in, I mean the flesh
of Christ and Holy Scripture. The flesh of Christ,
the Incarnate Word, is beyond all question a veil.[2]
How much did it hide, even while to some it revealed God. How few knew what He was: how
many misunderstood Him. And how inconsistent
did that feeble form appear with the truth that it
was God's chosen dwelling-place. The apparent inconsistency may be gathered from the fact that those
to whom He came stumbled at it. And from that
day to this that human form, that birth of a woman,
that growth in years and stature, those tears, that
sweat, that weariness, those bitter cries, those members of shame, that dying life, all this, or part of
this, has to the eye of sense seemed so inconsistent
with divinity, that thousands have denied that that
Form was or could be a revelation of God, even

[1] Psalm lxxiii. 3–17.   [2] Heb. x. 20.

while they allow that it has done what mere humanity never did. The fact is, it was, and was intended to be, a veil as well as a revelation: and as such there could not but be apparent contradiction.

The same is true of Scripture, that is, the written word, which like Nature has gone through six days of change, and like Christ's flesh has grown in wisdom and stature here. Throughout it is a veil while it is a revelation; and therefore, like Nature, Providence, and the flesh of Christ, it is and must be open to the same reproach, not only of inconsistency, but of setting forth unworthy and even untrue statements of God. For indeed Scripture is a veil, which when taken in the letter, that is, as it appears to sense, makes out God to be just as far from what He really is as Nature and Providence seem to make Him; and yet all the while it reveals Him also, as nothing else has ever revealed Him. For though in Christ's flesh the revelation is complete spite of the veil, its very completeness and compactness keep us from seeing the various parts, which are set before us in Holy Scripture piecemeal,[1] and in a way that neither Nature nor Providence at present shew Him to us. For the law and the prophets tell us more of God and of His purposes, as to the restitution of all things and the promised times of rest and sabbath, than Nature yet declares to our present understanding; though indeed Nature may

[1] πολυμερ ὼς καὶ πολυτρόπως.—Heb. i. 1.

be, and probably is, saying far more to us than any
mere human eye or ear has yet apprehended.

Now if Nature and Providence, Christ's flesh and
Scripture, have all this same characteristic peculiarity
of being veils as well as revelations, and are therefore open to the charge of inconsistency, as read
by sense, seeming to declare what is opposed to fact,
may we not conclude that they have all come from
the same Hand, especially when it is seen that the
apparent contradictions, which are found in any of
these revelations, like the tabernacle veil, invariably
cover some deeper truth, which cannot safely be expressed, to fallen men at least, in any other way.

(3) The deeper question, why God has thus revealed Himself should not be passed by; for it opens
the heart of God. God alone of all teachers has had
two methods, law and gospel, flesh and spirit,—one
working where we are, the other to bring us in rest
where He is,—one to be done away, the other to
abide,[1]—which at least looks like inconsistency. The
reason is that God is love, and that in no other way
could He ever have reached us where we were, or
brought us where He is. God therefore was willing
to seem inconsistent, and for awhile to come into
man's likeness, to bring man back to His likeness.
Here is the reason for law before gospel, for Christ's
flesh before His Spirit, for all the different dispensations, and for all the types and shadows which for

---

[1] 2 Cor. iii. 11.

awhile veiled while they revealed God's living Word. Here is the reason for the human form of the Divine Word in Scripture. Had that Word come to us as it is in itself, we should no more have apprehended or seen it than we see God. Had it come to us even in angelic form, only a very few, the pure and thoughtful, ever could have received it. But it stooped to reveal itself to creatures through a creature, and to come to us out of the heart of man in truly human form, so that all men, Gentile or Jew, polished or savage, might through its perfect humanity be able to receive it. God more than any of His most loving servants has become a Jew to gain the Jews, and weak to gain the weak, and under law to gain those under law; because He is love, and love must sacrifice itself, if by any means it can save and bless others. If therefore men are in the flesh, God comes to them in flesh; if they are in darkness and shadows, God comes for them into the shadows; because they cannot comprehend the light, and because the darkness and light are both alike to Him.[1]

If this is not the way of His revelation, how, I ask, has He ever revealed Himself? Will any dare to say that He has not revealed Himself? Has God who is love been content to leave poor man in perfect ignorance? Or if He has told man what He is, as most surely He has, how has He done so?

[1] Psalm cxxxix. 12.

Did He, does He, can He, plainly tell out to all
what He is? And if He did not, why did He not?
Why have men always heard God first speaking in
law before a gospel dawned on them? Why must it
be so, or at least why does He allow it? Is it a
mistake of His, which we must avoid, when we
attempt to make Him known; or shall we be wise,
if, in doing what He is doing, that is, in revealing
Him, we imitate His way of revelation? Surely
from the days of Adam, seeing what man is, and our
delusions about Him, God must have desired, and
we know has desired, to make Himself known; and
being Almighty, All-wise, and All-loving, surely He
has taken the best method of doing it. Again I ask,
how has He done it, how must He do it, man being
what he is? Could God consistently with our
salvation have done it otherwise than it has been
done? To shew Himself as He is would to man be
no shewing of Him. It was needful that He should
shew Himself under the forms and limitations of
that creature in and to whom He sought to reveal
Himself, that is by shadows before light, by law
before gospel, by a letter before a quickening spirit,
in a word, by the humiliation of His eternal Word
stooping to come out of man's heart and in human
form.

And yet this could not be done without the Truth
by its very humanity laying itself open to the charge
of being merely human and not divine, and to the
humiliation of being rejected for having our infirm-

ities upon it. Love can bear all this, and God is love, and the truth can bear it, for truth must conquer all things. And therefore while it submits to take a human form, in which it can be judged and die, (for it must die, and to some of us has died, in the form we first apprehended it,—a trial of faith sooner or later to be known by all disciples, who, like apostles of old in the same strait, are sorely perplexed at this dying, for they have trusted that this is He which should have redeemed Israel,—) it must also live and rise again, and glorify that human form for ever. But because it has thus stooped to come in human form, out of the heart of man, even as Christ came forth from Mary, for us, therefore like Him it shall be stripped and mocked. But those who are stripping it know not what they do.

§ II. *The Testimony of Scripture.*

I pass on now from the nature of Scripture to its teachings as to the destiny of the human race, and more especially of those who here either reject or never hear the gospel. I feel how solemn the enquiry is, not only because no subject can be of greater moment, but because what appears to me to be the truth differs from those conclusions which have been received by the majority of Christians. Believing, however, that the Holy Scripture, under God and His Spirit's teaching, is the final appeal in all controversies,—regarding it as the unexhausted mine from

whence the unsearchable riches of Christ have yet
still more to be dug out,—acknowledging no authority against its conclusions, and with the deepest
conviction that one jot and one tittle shall in no wise
pass from the law till all be fulfilled,—I turn to it on
this as on every other point, to listen and bow to its
decisions. And knowing, for by grace this Word is no
stranger to me, that like Christ's flesh it is a veil as
well as a revelation,—knowing that it has many
things to say which we cannot bear at first, and that,
if taken partially or in the letter, it may appear to
teach what is directly opposed to Christ's mind and
to its true meaning;—in this like not a few of Christ's
own words, as when He said, " He that hath no sword,
let him sell his garment and buy one;"[1] and again,
"Destroy this temple, and in three days I will raise
it up;"[2] and again, "He that eateth me shall live by
me;"[3] and again, "Our friend Lazarus sleepeth;"[4] all
of which were misunderstood by not a few of those
who first heard these words from Christ's own mouth;
—knowing too that the words of Holy Scripture, in
many places where they seem contradictory, and in
its "dark sayings,"[5] and "things hard to be understood,"[6] ever cover some deep and blessed mystery,
I see that the question is, not what this or that text,
taken by itself or in the letter, seems to say at first
sight, but rather what is the mind of God, and what

[1] S. Luke xxii. 36.   [2] S. John ii. 19.
[3] S. John vi. 57.   [4] S. John xi. 11.
[5] Psalm lxxviii. 2; Prov, i. 6.   [6] 2 S. Pet. iii. 16.

the real meaning in His Word of any apparent inconsistency. If I err in attempting to answer this, my error will, I trust, provoke some better exposition of God's truth. If what I see is truth, like His coming who was the Truth, it must bring glory to God on high and on earth peace and goodwill to men.

What then does Scripture say on this subject? Its testimony appears at first sight contradictory. Not only is there on the one hand law, condemning all, while on the other hand there is the gospel, with good news for every one; but further there are direct statements as to the results of these, which at first sight are apparently irreconcileable. First our Lord calls His flock " a little flock,"[1] and states distinctly that " many are called, but few are chosen ;"[2] that "strait is the gate and narrow is the way that leadeth unto life,[3] and few there be that find it ;"[4] that "many shall seek to enter in, and shall not be able;"[5] that while " he that believeth on the Son hath everlasting life,[6] he that believeth not the Son shall not see life, but the wrath of God abideth on him ;"[7] that " the wicked shall go away into everlasting punishment,"[8] " prepared for the devil and his angels ;"[9] " the resurrection of damnation ;"[10] " the

---

[1] S. Luke xii. 32.
[2] S. Matt. xx. 16, and xxii. 14.
[3] εἰς τὴν ζωήν.
[4] S. Matt. vii. 14.
[5] S. Luke xiii. 24.
[6] ζωὴν αἰώνιον.
[7] S. John iii. 36.
[8] S. Matt. xxv. 46; κόλασιν αἰώνιον.
[9] S. Matt. xxv. 41.
[10] S. John v. 29.

damnation of hell,"[1] "where their worm dieth not, and the fire is not quenched;"[2] that though "every word against the Son of Man may be forgiven, the sin against the Holy Ghost shall not be forgiven, neither in this world,[3] nor in that which is to come;"[4] and that of one at least it is true, that "good had it been for that man if he had not been born."[5]

These are the words of Christ Himself, and they are in substance repeated just as strongly by His Apostles. St. Paul declares that while some are "saved" by the gospel, others "perish;"[6] that "many walk whose end is destruction;"[7] that "the Lord Jesus shall be revealed, in flaming fire taking vengeance on them that know not God, and obey not the gospel of our Lord Jesus Christ, who shall be punished with everlasting destruction[8] from the presence of the Lord, and from the glory of His power, when He shall come to be glorified in His saints, and to be admired in all them that believe in that day."[9] To the Hebrews he says, "If we sin wilfully after that we have received the knowledge of the truth, there remaineth no more sacrifice for sins, but a certain fearful looking for of judgment and fiery indignation, which shall devour the adversaries;"[10] that "it is a fearful thing to fall into the hands of the living

---

[1] S. Matt. xxiii. 33.
[2] *ἐν τούτῳ τῷ αἰῶνι.*
[3] S. Matt. xxvi. 24.
[4] Phil. iii. 19.
[5] 2 Thess. i. 8–10.
[6] S. Mark ix. 44.
[7] S. Matt. xii. 32.
[8] 2 Cor. ii. 15.
[9] *ὄλεθρον αἰώνιον.*
[10] Heb. x. 26, 27.

God," [1] for " our God is a consuming fire." [2] St. Peter
repeats the same doctrine, that " judgment must
begin at the house of God, and if it first begin at
us, what shall the end be of them that obey not
the gospel of God; for if the righteous scarcely be
saved, where shall the ungodly and the sinner appear ?" [3]   He further says of " false teachers," who
" deny the Lord that bought them," that they " shall
bring upon themselves swift destruction," and, like
the cities of Sodom and Gomorrha, " shall utterly
perish in their own corruption." [4]   St. John's words
are at least as strong, that " the fearful, and unbelieving, and murderers, and whoremongers, and sorcerers, and idolaters, and all liars, shall have their
place in the lake which burneth with fire and brim
stone, which is the second death ;" [5] and that " those
who worship the beast, and his image, shall drink of
the wine of the wrath of God, and shall be tormented
with fire and brimstone in the presence of the holy
angels and the presence of the Lamb, and they have
no rest day nor night, and the smoke of their torment ascendeth up for ever and ever." [6]

Words could not well be stronger. The difficulty
is that all this is but one side of Scripture, which in
other places seems to teach a very different doctrine.
For instance, there are first the words of God Him-

---

[1] Heb. x. 31.
[2] Heb. xii. 29.
[3] 1 S. Pet. iv. 17; 18.
[4] 2 S. Pet. ii. 1, 3, 6, 12.
[5] Rev. xxi. 8.
[6] Rev. xiv. 9, 10, 11 ; εἰς αἰῶνας αἰώνων.

self, repeated again and again by those same Apostles
whom I have just quoted, that " in Abraham's seed
all the kindreds of the earth shall be blessed ; "[1]
words which St. Peter expounds to mean that there
shall be " a restitution of all things," adding that
" God hath spoken of this by the mouth of all His
holy prophets since the world began."[2]   St. Paul
further declares this wondrous " mystery of God's
will, that He hath purposed in Himself, according
to His good pleasure, to rehead[3] and reconcile[4] unto
Himself, in and by Christ, all things, whether they
be things in heaven," that is the spirit-world, where
the conflict with Satan yet is,[5] " or things on earth,"
that is this outward world, where death now reigns,
and where even God's elect are by nature children
of wrath, even as other men.[6]   Further St. Paul
asserts that " all creation, which now groans, shall
be delivered from the bondage of corruption, into
the glorious liberty of the children of God."[7]   In
another place he declares, that " God was in Christ
reconciling the world unto Himself,"[8] and that Christ
" took our flesh and blood, through death to destroy
him that had the power of death, that is, the devil ;"[9]
that " if by the offence of one many be dead, much

[1] Gen. xii. 3 ; xxii. 18 ; Acts iii. 25 ; Gal. iii. 8.
[2] Acts iii. 21.   [3] ἀνακεφαλαιώσασθαι.
[4] ἀποκατάλλαξαι, to reconcile back again.
[5] Rev. xii. 7.   [6] Eph. i. 9, 10 ; Col. i. 20 ; Eph. ii. 3.
[7] Rom. viii. 19–23.   [8] 2 Cor. v. 19.
[9] Heb. ii. 14.

more the grace of God and the gift by grace, which is by one man, Jesus Christ, hath abounded unto many :" [1] that " therefore as by the offence of one, or by one offence, judgment came on all to condemnation, even so by the righteousness of one, or by one righteousness, the free gift should come on all unto justification of life," while " they which receive abundance of grace, and of the gift of righteousness, shall reign in life by one, Jesus Christ ; " [2] that " as sin hath reigned unto death, so grace might reign unto eternal life," yea, that " where sin abounded, grace did yet much more abound." [3] To another church he states the same doctrine, that " as in Adam all die, even so in Christ shall all be made alive ; " [4] and that " the end " shall not come " till all are subject to Him," that " God may be," not all in some, but " all in all ; for He must reign till He hath put all enemies under His feet ; the last enemy that shall be destroyed is death." [5] So he says again, " Blessed be the God and Father of our Lord Jesus Christ, who hath blessed us with all spiritual blessings in heavenly places in Christ, . . . that in the dispensation of the fulness of times He might gather together in one all things in Christ, both which are in heaven and which are in earth, even in Him." [6] To the same purpose he writes in another epistle, " that at, (or in,[7]) the name of Jesus,

---

[1] Rom. v. 15. [2] Rom. v. 17, 18. [3] Rom. v. 20, 21.
[4] 1 Cor. xv. 22. [5] 1 Cor. xv. 24–28. [6] Eph. i. 3–10.
[7] ἐν τῷ ὀνόματι: cf. S. John xiv. 13, 14 ; and xvi. 23, 24.

(that is Saviour,) every knee shall bow, of things in heaven, and things on earth, and things under the earth ; and that every tongue shall confess that Jesus Christ is Lord, to the glory of God the Father;"[1] " for to this end Christ both died, and rose, and revived, that He might be Lord both of the dead and living."[2] He further declares that " for this sake he suffers reproach, because he hopes in the living God, who is the Saviour of all men, specially of those who believe;"[3] that this God " will have all men to be saved, and to come to the knowledge of the truth ; " that therefore " thanksgivings as well as prayers should be made for all," because there is " a ransom for all, to be testified in due time ; "[4] and lastly that " God hath concluded all in unbelief, that He might have mercy upon all."[5]   The beloved Apostle St. John repeats the same doctrine, that " the Father sent the Son to be the Saviour of the world ;"[6] " for God sent not His Son into the world to condemn the world, but that the world by Him might be saved;"[7] further He teaches that the Only-Begotten Son " is the propitiation, not for our sins only, but also for the sins of the whole world:"[8] that He is " the Lamb of God, which taketh away the sin of the world,"[9] and " was revealed for this very purpose that He might destroy the works of the devil,"[10]

[1] Phil. ii. 10, 11.   [2] Rom. xiv. 9.   [3] 1 Tim. iv. 10.
[4] 1 Tim. ii. 1–6.   [5] Rom. xi. 32.   [6] 1 S. John iv. 14.
[7] S. John iii. 17.   [8] 1 S. John ii. 2.
[9] S. John i. 29.   [10] 1 S. John iii. 8.

and that, as a result, " there shall be no more death, nor sorrow, nor pain, because all things are made new, and the former things are passed away."[1] For " the Father loveth the Son, and hath given all things into His hand :"[2] and the Son Himself declares, " All that the Father giveth me shall come to me ; and him that cometh to me I will in no wise cast out. For I came down from heaven, not to do mine own will, but the will of Him that sent me. And this is the Father's will, which hath sent me, that of all which He hath given me I should lose nothing, but should raise it up again at the last day."[3] And again He says, " And I, if I be lifted up from the earth, will draw all men unto me." [4]

Now is not this apparent contradiction,—few finding the way of life, and yet in Christ all made alive,— God's elect a little flock, and yet all the kindreds of the earth blessed in Abraham's seed,—mercy upon all, and yet eternal punishment,—the restitution of all things, and yet eternal destruction,—the wrath of God for ever, and yet all things reconciled to Him,— eternal fire prepared for the devil and his angels, and yet the destruction through death, not of the works of the devil only, but of him who has the power of death, that is the devil,—the second death and the lake which burneth with fire, and yet no more death or curse, but all things subdued by Christ, and God

---

[1] Rev. xxi. 4, 5 ; and see Rev. v. 13.
    S. John vi. 37–39.

[2] S. John iii. 35.

[4] S. John xii. 32.

all in all. What can this contradiction mean? Is
there any key, and if so, what is it, to this mystery?

The common answer is, that these opposing words
only mean, that some are saved and some are lost
for ever; that the saved are the elect of this and
other dispensations, who as compared with the world
have hitherto been but a little flock; but that,
though as yet few have found the strait and narrow
way, all nations shall be saved in the Millennium;
further that though we read, "There shall be no
more death," yet, since the wrath of God is for ever,
there must be eternal death, (words by the way not
to be found in all Scripture,) and that this death
consists in never ending torments, so endless that
after the lapse of ages on ages the punishment of the
wicked shall be no nearer its end than when it first
commenced; that therefore the words, "In Christ shall
all be made alive," only mean that all who are here
in Christ shall be made alive; that the Lamb of
God, though willing to be, is not really the Saviour of
the world, but only of those who are not of the world,
but chosen out of it; that instead of taking away the
sin of the world, He only takes away the sin of those
who here believe in Him; that all things therefore
shall not be reconciled to God, and that "the restitution of all things," whatever it may mean, does not
mean the reconciliation to God of all men.

This is the approved teaching of Christendom;
this is the orthodox solution of the mystery; the
simple objection to which is, that in asserting one

side of Scripture, it is obliged, not only to ignore and deny the other side, but to represent God in a character absolutely opposed to that in which the gospel exhibits Him. Nor does it meet the difficulty to say, as some have said, that though a large proportion of mankind are lost for ever, the greater part will probably be saved, inasmuch as at least one-half of the race die in infancy, whose sin is perfectly atoned for by Christ's sacrifice. What is this but saying, that, if evil has fair play, it will overmatch all that God can do to meet and remedy it? Is this indeed the glad tidings of great joy? Is this the glorious gospel of the blessed God? Is it not simply a misapprehension of God's purpose, arising out of some mystery connected with the method of our redemption? But "the Scripture cannot be broken" thus.[1] Not a few therefore have confessed that there is some difficulty here, which as yet they cannot solve or reconcile. Is the mystery beyond our present light? or is there any, and if so, what is the, key to it?

The truth which solves the riddle is to be found in those same Scriptures which seem to raise the difficulty, and lies in the mystery of the will of our ever blessed God as to the process and stages of redemption :—

(1) First, His will by some to bless and save others; by a first-born seed, "the first-born from the dead,"[2] to save and bless the later-born :—

[1] S. John x. 35.   [2] Col. i. 18.

(2) His will therefore to work out the redemption of the lost by successive ages or dispensations, or, to use the language of St. Paul, "according to the purpose of the ages :" [1]—and

(3) Lastly, His will (thus meeting the nature of our fall,) to make death, judgment, and destruction, the means and way to life, acquittal, and salvation ; in other words, " through death to destroy him that has the power of death, that is the devil, and to deliver them who through fear of death were all their lifetime subject to bondage." [2]

These truths throw a flood of light on Scripture, and enable us at once to see order and agreement, where without this light there seems perplexing inconsistency. We should of course get deeper views, if, instead of starting from the fall, and merely asking what is declared as to its results and remedy, we began with God, and enquired what He has revealed as to His end in making man, and how far, if at all, His purpose in creation is or has been frustrated in any way. Did the entrance of sin change or affect God's plan ? Was redemption only an after-thought to meet an undesigned or undesired difficulty ? What was the object of the Incarnation ? On what grounds, and for what end, is judgment committed to the Son of Man ? What was intended to be accomplished by the first and second death ? These are questions which must meet us, if we think of God and of His thoughts, and give Him credit for having had a

[1] Eph. iii. 11.   [2] Heb. ii. 14.

purpose in creation. Christ is the answer to them all; and His Word contains, though under a veil, the perfect key to these and all mysteries; though in His Word, as in His works, the open secret is unseen, and His wisdom, as in the wondrous laws of light, may be all around us and yet for ages undiscovered. For God's sons still think it strange and even unbecoming to enquire "what is the breadth and length and depth and height" of their heavenly Father's purpose. But for our present object we need not ask all this. It is enough to begin with ourselves as fallen, and to enquire what Scripture reveals as to the results of our fall, and of the remedy. We shall see how God's will, as witnessed, first in the " law of the first-fruits " and " first-born," then in the " purpose of the ages," and lastly in the mystery of " death " and " judgment," as it is opened by Christ's cross and resurrection, clears away all that looks like contradiction between " mercy upon all" and yet " eternal judgment." By this light we see more fully God's purpose in Christ, and how He is " Saviour of all men, specially of those that believe ;"[1] how " to those who overcome He will grant to sit with Him on His throne,"[2] and make them partakers of all His glories ; while others, not partakers of the first resurrection, are only brought to God by the resurrection of judgment, that is by the judgments of the coming age or ages. But till God opens all is shut. A man can receive nothing

[1] 1 Tim. iv. 10.   [2] Rev. iii. 21.

except it be given him from above. "Eye hath not seen, nor ear heard, neither have entered into the heart of man, the things which God hath prepared for them that love Him. But God hath revealed them to us by His Spirit, for the Spirit searcheth all things, yea, the deep things of God. For who knoweth the things of man but the spirit of man which is in him? Even so the things of God knoweth no man but the Spirit of God."[1]

Let us look then in order at each of these three points :—

(1) First, the purpose of God by the first-fruits or first-born to save and bless the later-born.

This, which is in fact the substance of the gospel, like all God's secrets, comes out by degrees. Scarcely to be discerned, though contained, in the first promise of the Woman's Seed,[2] it shines out brightly in the covenant made with Abraham :—" In thy seed shall all the kindreds of the earth be blessed ;"[3] for the seed, in whom all the kindreds of the earth are blessed, must be distinct from, and blessed prior to, those nations to whom according to God's purpose in due time it becomes a blessing. This purpose is then revealed with fuller detail in the law of the first-fruits and the first-born,[4] though here the veil of type and shadow hides from most the face of Moses. But in Christ the purpose is unveiled for ever, and the mystery, by the first-born to save

---

[1] 1 Cor. ii. 9–11   [3] Gen. iii. 15.
[2] Gen. xxii. 18   [4] Rom. xi. 16.

others, is by the Holy Ghost made fully manifest. Christ, says the Apostle, is the promised Seed,[1] the First-born,[2] and in and through Him endless blessing shall flow down on the later-born.

Now Christ, as Paul shews, is first-born in a double sense. He is first-born from above, first out of life, for He is the Only-Begotten Son of God, begotten of the Father before all worlds; " for by Him were all things created, which are in heaven and which are in earth, visible and invisible, whether they be thrones, or dominions, or principalities, or powers, all things were created by Him and for Him, and He is before all things, and by Him all things consist."[3] But He is more than this, for He is also " first-born from the dead," first out of death, " that in all things He might have the pre-eminence;"[4] and it is in this relation, as first-born from the dead, that He is Head of the Church, and first-fruits of the creature. All things are indeed of God, but it is no less true also that all things are by man; as it is written, " Since by man came death, by man came also the resurrection of the dead:"[5] Therefore as by one first-born death came into the world, so by another first-born shall it be for ever overthrown. Herein is love indeed, that the whole remedy for sin shall come through man, even as the sin did. Thus not only is there salvation for man, but by man, for the Eternal Son is Son of Man also; who by a birth

[1] Gal. iii. 16.   [2] Col. i. 18.   [3] Col. i. 15–17.
[4] Col. i. 18.   [5] 1 Cor. xv. 21.

in the flesh has come into our lot, that by another
birth out of the grave He might also be the first-
born from the dead; and it is in virtue of this
relation that He fulfils for us all those offices which
are included in the word Redeemer.   The law of
Moses is most instructive here: for while it is true
that the letter of that law cannot be explained but
by the gospel, it is no less true that the gospel in its
breadth and depth cannot be set forth save by the
figures of the law, each jot of which covers some
blessed mystery.

What then does the law teach us of this First-born
from the dead; for be it observed it is ever the
first-born from the grave that the law speaks of,—
therefore the woman's, not the man's, first-born,
"the male which first openeth the womb,"[1] who
might, though not necessarily, be also the father's
first-born.   For the law, as made for sinners only,[2]
needed not to speak of the First-born as proceeding
out of God, but only of the First-born as raised up
by Him out of the grave and barren womb of this
present fallen and unclean nature.   According to the
law, the First-born had the right, though it might be
lost, of being priest and king, that is of interceding
for and ruling over their younger brethren;[3] on him
devolved the duty of Goel or Redeemer, to redeem
a brother who had waxen poor, and sold himself

[1] Exod. xiii. 12; xxxiv. 19; Numb. iii. 12, 13.
[2] 1 Tim. i. 9.
[3] Exod. xiii. 2; xxiv. 5; Numb. iii. 12, 13 viii. 16; 1 Chron. v. I, 2.

unto a stranger; to avenge his blood, to raise up
seed to the dead, and to redeem the inheritance, if
at any time it were lost or alienated.[1] To sustain
these duties God gave him a double portion.[2] Need
I point out how Christ fulfils these particulars; how
as first out of the grave, that " barren womb, which
cries, Give, give,"[3] He is the First-born through
whom the blessing reaches us? In this sense no
Christian doubts that God's purpose is by the First-
born from the dead to save and bless the later-born.

But the truth goes further still, for there are
others beside the Lord who are both " first-born "
and " Abraham's seed," who must therefore in their
measure share this same honour with and under
Christ, and in whom, as "joint-heirs with Him,"[4]
the promise must be fulfilled, that in them " all the
kindreds of the earth shall be blessed."[5] This glorious truth, though of the very essence of the gospel,
which announces salvation to the world through the
promised seed of Abraham, is even yet so little seen
by many of Abraham's seed, that not a few of the
children of the promise speak and act as if Christ
and His body only should be saved, instead of rejoicing that they are also the appointed means of
saving others. Even of the elect, few see that they
are elect to the birthright, not to be blessed only,

---

[1] Lev. xxv. 47, 48; Deut. xix. 4-12; Gen. xxxviii. 8; Deut. xxv.
5-10; Ruth iv. 6-10; Lev. xxv. 25; Ruth ii. 20.
[2] Deut. xxi. 17.
[3] Prov. xxx. 15, 16.   [4] Rom. viii. 17.   [5] Gen. xxii. 18.

but to be a blessing; as first-born with Christ to
share the glory of kingship and priesthood with
Him, not only to rule and intercede for their younger
and later-born brethren, but to avenge their blood,
to raise up seed to the dead, and in and through
Christ, their life and head, to redeem their lost inheritance.   Thank God, if the elect know not their
double portion, God knows and keeps it for them,
and will in due time, spite of their blindness, fulfil
His purpose in and by them.   But surely it is a
reproach to the heirs, that they know not their
Father's purpose, and that through not knowing it
they bear so imperfect a testimony as to His goodwill to all His fallen creatures.

The whole old law beams with light upon this
point, not only in its ordinances and appointments
as to the first-born and their double portion, but
also in the details of the oblation of the first-fruits,
which is only another aspect and presentation of the
same mystery.   The seed of nature figures the seed
of grace, and the first-fruits of the one are but the
shadow of the other, that " seed of the kingdom "
which is first ripe for heaven, ripened by the true
Sun[1] and Light[2] and Air,[3] of which the sun and
light and air of present nature in all their wondrous
workings are the silent but ceaseless witnesses.   The
type is very full and striking here; for the law,
which required the first-fruits, speaks of a double

[1] Psa. lxxxiv. 11.   [2] S. John viii. 12.   [3] S. John iii. 8.

first-fruits.[1] The first, the sheaf or handful of un-leavened ears, the first to spring up out of the dark and cold earth, which lay the shortest time under its darkness, soonest ripe to be a sacrifice on God's altar, was offered at the first great feast of the year, the feast of unleavened bread, which is the Pass-over.[2] The other, which are also called " first-fruits," were offered in the form of leavened cakes, fifty days later at Pentecost.[3] Both in the law are distinctly called " first-fruits," though they are distinguished by a separate name, the ears at Passover being called *Rashith*, the leavened cakes at Pentecost, *Bicou-rim*;[4] to which the gospel exactly agrees, saying, " Christ the First-fruits,"[5] and " we a kind of first-fruits :"[6] Christ " the First-born,"[7] and we "the church of the first-born ; "[8] words which carry with them blessings unspeakable, "for if the first-fruit be holy, the lump is also holy,"[9] the offering of the first-fruits to God being accepted as the sanctifica-tion and consecration of the whole coming harvest.

Need I say Christ is the Paschal first-fruits and first-born. The day of His resurrection was the very

---

[1] Lev. xxiii. 10, 17.

[2] Lev. xxiii. 10, 11 ; S. Luke xxii. 1.   [3] Lev. xxiii. 17.

[4] Rashith, or " the beginning," the title given in the law to the Paschal first-fruits, is the very word used by St. Paul of Christ in the passage already quoted,—" He is the head of the body, the Church, who is *the beginning*, the first-born from the dead," &c.—Col. i. 18.

[5] 1 Cor. xv. 23.

[6] S. James, 1. 18. See also Rev. xiv. 4.   [7] Col. i. 18.

[8] Heb. xii. 23.   [9] Rom. xi. 16.

day of the offering of the first first-fruits.[1] But who
are those, who, as leavened bread, share the honour
with and under Him of being the Pentecostal first-
fruits? Who with Christ and through Christ are
Abraham's seed?

First, the Jew is Abraham's seed,—"the people
that dwell alone, and are not reckoned among the
nations;"[2] and though "all are not Israel who are
of Israel,"[3] Scripture will indeed be broken, if
Israel is not again grafted in; when, if the casting
away of them has been the riches of the world, the
receiving of them, as St. Paul says, shall be life from
the dead.[4] "Israel is my son, my first-born, saith
the Lord."[5] All nations, therefore, shall yet be
blessed in them. They are indeed only the earthly
first-born, but as first-born, though of the least-

[1] These first first-fruits were offered " on the morrow after the
sabbath " after the Passover, (Lev. xxiii. 11,) that is the very day,
" the first day of the week," on which Christ rose from the dead. I
may, perhaps, add here, for it is most noteworthy, that in 2 Sam. xxi. 9,
we are told that "all the seven sons of Saul fell together in the days
of harvest, in the first day, in the beginning of barley harvest;"
that is they fell on the day of the first first-fruits. The books of
Kings, where this is recorded, are the books of Rule, shewing out
in mystery all the forms of Rule under which God's elect have been
either in bondage or liberty. The first form of rule is Saul, whose
name means Death or Hell. He is the figure of the rule under
which we all are at first, while "death reigns" by God's appointment. (Rom. v. 14, 17.) All his seven sons, that is, the fruits of
death, fall in one day, under the reign of David, that is the Beloved ; that one day being the sacred day of the Paschal first-fruits,
the day of Christ's resurrection.

[2] Numb. xxiii. 9.
[3] Rom. ix. 6.
[4] Rom. xi. 15.
[5] Exod. iv. 22.

loved wife, they must in their own sphere possess
the double blessing ;[1] being not blessed only, but
made blessings to the nations, whose conversion the
Church is rightly looking for, but whom the Church
shall not convert ; for the conversion of the nations
is already promised to Israel, who, dwellers among
all nations, yet not of them, are even now being
trained and prepared for this, and who at their conversion, converted like Paul, who is their type,[2] not
by the knowledge of Christ in humiliation, but by
the revelation of His heavenly glory, shall like Paul
become apostles to the Gentiles, " priests to the Lord
and ministers to our God,"[3] to all upon the earth.[4]

[1] Deut. xxi. 15, 16.

[2] 1 Tim. i. 16; πρὸς ὑποτύπωσιν τῶν μελλόντων πιστεύειν—
literally, " for a type of those who shall hereafter believe." Paul is
not a type of "the first trusters in Christ," (see Eph. i. 12,) that is
of believers now, but of " those who shall hereafter believe," when
Christ reveals Himself in glory ; and his peculiar experience, for he
was " as one born out of due time," (1 Cor. xv. 8,) as well as his conversion in an extraordinary way by a sight of Christ's glory, were
earnests and figures of what should be wrought in Israel, who shall
be converted to Christ in a similar and no less sudden manner.
Isa. lxvi. 8, 12, 18, 19.

[3] Exod. xix. 6 ; Isa. lxi. 6.

[4] Very wonderful is the statement in the Song of Moses, (Deut.
xxxii. 8,) addressed both to the heavens and earth, which declares
that, "when the Most High divided to the nations their inheritance,
when He separated the sons of Adam, *He set the bounds of the peoples
according to the number of the children of Israel.*" Now the number
of the children of Israel, when they went down into Egypt, was
seventy ; (Gen. xlvi. 27 ; Exod. i. 5 ; Deut. x. 22 ;) and, answering
to this, in Gen. x., which gives the account of the peoples to whom
the earth was divided after the flood, we read of seventy heads of

But (and this concerns us) the Church is also
Abraham's seed; for, as St. Paul says, "If ye be
Christ's, ye are Abraham's seed, and heirs according
to the promise."[1]   To the Church therefore belongs
the same promise, as first-fruits with Christ, not to
be blessed only, but to be a blessing, in its own
heavenly and spiritual sphere.   For if the Jew on
earth shall be a "kingdom of priests," what is our
hope but to be also heavenly "kings and priests,"[2]
as "kings," for the Lord shall say, "Be thou over
five cities,"[3] to rule and order in the coming age
what requires order; not only with Christ to "judge
the world,"[4] but to be "equal unto the angels" and
to "judge angels;"[5] as "priests," for a priest is "for
those out of the way,"[6] to minister to those who yet
are out of the way.   This is the Church's calling, to
do Christ's works, as He said, "He that believeth on
me, the works that I do shall he do also;"[7] with
Him to be both prophet, priest, and king, and this,
not here only in these bodies of humiliation, but
when changed in His presence to bear His image
and do His works with Him.   Christ barely entered
on His priestly work till He had passed through death

nations.   Surely there is a secret here, connected with Christ's mission of the Seventy, which was distinct from and followed the mission
of the Apostolic Twelve, by whom and under whom the Church is
gathered out.   See S. Luke x. 1.
  [1] Gal. iii. 29.   [2] Rev. i. 6; v. 10.
  [3] S. Luke xix. 17, 19; Psa. xlv. 16.
  [4] 1 Cor. vi. 2.   [5] S. Luke xx. 36; 1 Cor. vi. 3.
  [6] Heb. v. 2.   [7] S. John xiv. 12.

and judgment;[1] so with those who are Christ's, their
death and resurrection shall only introduce them to
fuller and wider service to lost ones, over whom
the Lord shall set them as His priests and kings,
until all things are restored and reconciled unto
Him. It is, alas, too true that of the Church's
sons, some like Esau shall sell their birthright for
some present good thing, and that in this age as in
the last some of the children of the kingdom shall
be cast out, while others from the east and from the
west press in and win the crown and kingdom; yet
an elect first-born shall surely be preserved, who are
sealed to this pre-eminence, to be priests to God and
rulers of their brethren. To whom, I ask, shall the
Church after death be priests? Shall it be to that
great mass of our fellow men, who have departed
hence in ignorance? Shall it be to "spirits in prison," such as those to whom after His death Christ
Himself once preached?[2] Shall not His saints, made
like Him, do the same works, still following Him,

---

[1] Heb. iv. 14; vii. 15–17; viii. 4, 6.

[2] 1 S. Peter iii, 18–20. This passage, I know, is called "difficult,"
that is, it is one which it is hard and even impossible fairly to reconcile with the views called Orthodox. The words, however, are not
difficult. They distinctly assert that our Lord went and preached
to the spirits in prison, who once had been disobedient in the days of
Noah. The "difficulty" is that Protestant orthodoxy has decided that
there can be no message of mercy to any after death. Protestant
commentators therefore have attempted to evade the plain statements
of this Scripture, and their forced and unnatural interpretations shew
how very strong the passage is against them. Any one who wishes
to see a summary of these interpretations may find them collected in

and with Him being priests to God? Will not their
glory be to rule and feed and enlighten and clothe
those who are committed to them, even as Christ
has fed and clothed them? For He is " King of
kings and Lord of lords," [1] words which indicate
the many kings and rulers under Him, of whom He
is Head, and whom He makes heads to others.

I should perhaps be going beyond my measure
were I to follow in detail all that the law says further
as to the first-fruits and the first-born; but I may
add here, that this same truth, that the first-blessed
must save others, is set forth, though in a slightly
different form, in the kindred law of redemption
touching the firstlings of beasts, whether clean or
unclean. The lamb redeems the ass.[2] So it must
be. The clean are called, and content, to be sacrifices. For the law of redemption, which is the law
of love, is this, that they who are first redeemed and
blessed must bless others. And this is their joy, to

Alford's Greek Testament, *in loco.* His own comment is as follows:
—" I understand these words to say, that our Lord, in his disembodied state, did go to the place of detention of departed spirits, and
did there announce His work of redemption, preach salvation, in fact,
to the disembodied spirits of those who refused to obey the voice of
God, when the judgment of the flood was hanging over them." The
fact, that in the Prayer-book these verses are appointed to be read
as the Epistle for Easter Even, that is for the day after the cruci-
fixion, and before the resurrection of our Lord, shews plainly enough
the judgment of the English Church as to the true sense and interpretation of this passage. The Early Fathers, almost without exception, understand it to speak of Christ's descent to Hades.

[1] 1 Tim. vi. 15.   [2] Exod. xiii. 12, 13.

be like Christ, that is to be channels of blessing to viler, weaker souls. For all higher and elder beings serve the lower and younger. The first-born therefore must serve and save others. Their calling is to be, like Christ, channels of blessing and life to thousands of later-born.

Such glories are in store, to be revealed when the two leavened cakes of first-fruits, then completed, shall together be offered up, in that great coming Pentecost, of which the fiery tongues of old, and the rushing wind, in the upper room were but the type and earnest: when the elect, Christ's mystic body, being raised with Him, the Head not born alone, but all the members with it, the Spirit shall be poured out upon all flesh, and, the first-fruits being safe, the harvest, already sanctified by the first-fruits, shall also begin to be gathered in. Oh glorious day, when our Lord and Head shall give of His treasure to His first-born, that they may with Him redeem all lands and all brethren;[1] when with Him they shall judge their captive brethren, who through their unbelief have lost their own inheritance. Then shall the laver be multiplied into "ten lavers,"[2] till the water of life become a "sea of crystal,"[3] large enough even for Babylon the great to sink into it, and to be found

---

[1] Lev. xxv. 25, 47, 48.

[2] Compare Exod. xxx. 18, which speaks of the wilderness, with 1 Kings vii. 38, 39, which describes the far larger provision made for cleansing in the glorious reign of the Man of Peace, the true Son of David.

[3] Compare 1 Kings vii. 38, 39; 2 Chron. iv. 2-6; and Rev. xv. 2.

no more at all for ever. Then shall the elect " run to and fro as sparks among the stubble ;"[1] and as all sparks or seeds of light, though they may come forth at long intervals from one another, are yet congenial, if they have come out of a common root,—as they can not only mingle rays with rays and embrace each other, but in virtue of a common nature have the same power of consuming and purifying that they come in contact with,— so shall Christ's members judge the world with Him, and consume the evil with that same fire which Christ came to cast into the earth, and with which He is yet pledged to baptize all nations. For our Lord, who gave Himself, with Himself will give us all things, grudging His children nothing of that inheritance He has obtained for them.

Here then is the key to one part of the apparent contradiction between " mercy upon all," and yet " the election" of a " little flock ;" between " all the kindreds of the earth blessed in Christ," and yet a " strait and narrow way" and " few finding it." Here is the answer to the question, " Wilt thou shew wonders to the dead ? Shall the dead arise and praise thee ? Shall thy loving-kindness be declared in the grave, or thy faithfulness in destruction ? Shall thy wonders be known in the dark, and thy righteousness in the land of forgetfulness?"[2] The first-born and first-fruits are the " few" and " little

[1] Wisdom iii. 7, 8.   [2] See Psa. lxxxviii. 1-12.

flock;" but these, though first delivered from the
curse, have a relation to the whole creation, which
shall be saved in the appointed times by the first-
born seed, that is by Christ and His body, through
those appointed baptisms, whether of fire or water,
which are required to bring about " the restitution of
all things." St. Paul expressly declares this when he
says, " Blessed be the God and Father of our Lord
Jesus Christ, who hath blessed us with all spiritual
blessings in heavenly places in Christ, . . . that in
the dispensation of the fulness of times He might
gather together in one all things in Christ, both
which are in heaven and which are in earth, even in
Him."[1] The Church, like Christ its Head, is itself
a great sacrament ; " an outward and visible sign of
an inward and spiritual grace given unto men ;
ordained by God Himself, as a means whereby they
may receive the same, and a pledge to assure them
thereof ;" and " the blessing" of the elect, " with all
spiritual blessings in heavenly places in Christ," is
but the means and pledge, as the Apostle says, of
wider blessing ; the means by which " in the dispensation of the fulness of times" God designs to "gather
together in one all things in Christ, whether they
be things which are in heaven or which are in earth,
even in Him ;" and the pledge that He both can and
will do it, as He has already done it in some of the

[1] Eph. i. 3–10. The same doctrine is stated in almost the same
words, chapter ii. 4–7.

weakest and the worst; for " God hath chosen the
base things of the world, yea and things which are
not;"[1] to shew to all that there are none so weak
but He can save, and none so vile, but He can
change and cleanse them.// Thus when " He comes
with ten thousands of His saints," He will not only
by them " convince all ungodly sinners of all their
hard speeches, which they have spoken against
Him;"[2]—for if the thief be saved, and the Magdalene
changed, who shall dare to say that the lost are
uncared for or beyond the reach of God's salvation;—
but He will by them also, as His royal priests, joint-
heirs with Christ, fulfil all that priestly work of judgment and purification by fire, which must be accomplished that all may be "subdued"[3] and "reconciled."[4]
To say that God saves only the first-born would be,
if it may be said, to make Him worse than even
Moloch, whose slaves devoted only their first-born to
the flames, founding this dreadful rite upon the true
tradition that the sacrifice of a first-born should
redeem the rest; a requirement, tender, as compared
with that which some ascribe to the God and Father
of our Lord Jesus, who, according to their view,
accepts the elect or first-born only, and leaves the
rest to torments endless and most agonizing.   The
gospel of God tells us of better things, of a sacrifice
indeed, even of God's Only-Begotten Son, who,

[1] 1 Cor. i. 27, 28.   [2] S. Jude 14, 15.
[3] 1 Cor. xv. 28.   [4] Col. i. 20.

because we were dead, came into our death to quicken us, who took on Him the darkness, and death, and curse, which bound and would have for ever held us, and broke through it in the power of His eternal life, not only reconciling us by His blood, but also shewing us by His death the way out of the bondage of sin and this world, and who having thus in His own person, as Man, broken through death, gives Himself now to as many as will receive and follow Him, that in and by His life they also in the same path may come forth as first-fruits and first-born from the dead with Him. But Scripture never says that these only shall be saved, but rather that "in this seed," whose portion as the first-born is double,[1] "all the kindreds of the earth shall be blessed."

I fear that the elect, instead of bearing this witness, have too often ignored and even contradicted it. And yet the fact, that the Church for many hundred years has had an All-Souls Day as well as an All-Saints Day in her Calendar, is itself a witness that she may have been teaching far more than some of her sons as yet have learnt from her. For why did the Church ordain a celebration for All-Souls as well as for All-Saints, but because, spite of her children's contradiction, she believed that like her Lord she is truly linked to all, and with Him is ordained at last to gather all. And why does All-Souls Day follow All-Saints,[2] but to declare that All

---

[1] Deut. xxi. 17.

[2] November 1st is All-Saints Day : November 2nd, All-Souls.

Saints should reach All Souls, going before them
indeed, yet going before to be a blessing to them.
For indeed All Saints are to All Souls as the first-
born to their younger brethren, elect to be both kings
and priests to them; or as the first-fruits to the
harvest, the pledge of what is to come, if not also
the means to bring it about in due season.   I know
of course, that, through the abuse of masses for the
dead, All-Souls Day has since the Reformation been
dropped out of the Calendar of our English Church.
I neither judge nor defend our Reformers for what
they did in a time of very great difficulty.   I only
say that the truth once taught by All-Souls Day, if
ever a truth, must be a truth for all generations.
And I thank God that the Church had, and yet has,
such a day; and that, if not with English saints
now living, yet "with all saints," as the Apostle
says, " we may be able to comprehend the breadth
and length and depth and height, and to know the
love of Christ, which passeth knowledge, that we
may be filled with (or into) all the fulness of God."[1]
And in faith of that love and fulness I look for the day
when All Souls shall become the inheritance and
prize and glory of All Saints, who by grace have
gone before them.

Our knowledge however of this or any other mystery will serve us nothing, yea be far worse than
nothing, if, instead of running for the prize which

[1] Eph. iii. 19.

the gospel sets before us, we sit down content merely
to understand how the apparent contradictions of
Scripture can be reconciled. Not so do the first-born
win the prize. Christ has shewn the way, and there
is no other. He died to live—He suffered to reign—
He humbled Himself; therefore God hath greatly
exalted Him.[1] If we be dead with Him, we shall
live with Him,—if we suffer, we shall reign with
Him,[2]—joint-heirs with Christ, if so be we suffer
with Him, that we may be glorified together.[3] Only
by the cross can the change be wrought in us, which
conforms us to Christ and His image,- -which makes
us, like Him, lambs for the slaughter,[4] and as such
fitted to bless and serve others. And as corn does
not grow by any thinking of the process; as gold is
not melted by any speculation of the nature of fire,
but by being cast into it; so the change required is
only wrought in us through that baptism of fire, which
is so sharp that even the blessed Paul could say, " If
in this life only we have hope in Christ, we are of all
men most miserable,"[5] a trial very different from
that of the mass of professors, who suffer no more
than the common lot of humanity. And indeed so
narrow is the way, and so strait is the gate, that
leadeth to the life and glory of the first-born, who
"follow the Lamb withersoever He goeth ;"[6] so entire
is the loss and renunciation of the things dear to the

[1] Phil. ii. 8, 9.
[2] 2 Tim. ii. 11, 12.
[3] Rom. viii. 17.
[4] Rom. viii. 36.
[5] 1 Cor. xv. 19.
[6] Rev xiv. 4.

old man, whose will is entranced by the things that
are seen and temporal; so bitter is the cross that few
can bear it, and pass willingly through the fires which
must be passed to win that "high calling."[1]　Here
is the patience of the saints, to bear that fire in and
by which the old Adam is dissolved and slain, out of
which they rise, through "blood and fire and pillars
of smoke," that is the Pentecostal offering,[2] as sacrifices to God, to stand as kings and priests before
Him.

(2) I pass on to shew that God's purpose, by the
first-born from the dead to bless the later-born,—as
it is written, "So in Christ shall all be made alive,"
—is fulfilled in successive worlds or ages,[3] or, to use
the language of St. Paul, " according to the purpose
of the ages,"[4] so that the dead are raised, not all together, but " Every man in his own order—Christ
the first-fruits—afterwards they that are Christ's at
His coming;"[5] which latter resurrection, though
after Christ's, is yet called " the resurrection from
among the dead,"[6] or " the first resurrection."[7]

Now it is simply matter of fact, that Christ, the
first of the first-fruits, through whom all blessing
reaches us, rose from the dead eighteen hundred
years ago, while the Church of the first-born, who
are also called first-fruits,[8] will not be gathered till

---

[1] Phil. iii. 8–14.　　[2] Acts ii. 19; Cant. iii. 6.
[3] *αἰῶνες.*　　[4] Eph. iii. 11; κατὰ πρόθεσιν τῶν αἰώνων.
[5] 1 Cor. xv. 23.　　[6] Phil. iii. 11; τὴν ἐξανάστασιν, κ.τ.λ.
[7] Rev. xx. 5.　　[8] S. James i. 18; Rev. xiv. 4.

the great Pentecost. Some are therefore freed from death before others; and even of the first-fruits, the Head of the body, as in every proper birth, is freed before the other members. So far it is clear that this purpose of God is wrought, not at once, but through successive ages. But this fact gives a hint of further mysteries, and some key to the "ages of ages,"[1] which we read of in the New Testament, during which the lost are yet held by or under death and judgment, while the saints share Christ's glory, as heirs of God, in subduing all things unto Him. The fall here gives us some shadow of the restoration. For just as in Adam, all do not come out of him or die at once, but descend from or through each other, and die generation after generation, though all fell and died in him when he fell and died, as part of him, and therefore partakers of his sad inheritance; so in Christ, though all have been made alive in Him by His resurrection, all are not personally brought into His life and light at once, but one after another, and the first-born before the later-born, according to God's good pleasure and eternal purpose.

The key here as elsewhere is to be found in the details of that law, of which "no jot or tittle shall pass till all be fulfilled;"[2] the appointed "times and seasons" of which, one and all, are the types or figures of the "ages" of the New Testament; for there is nothing in the gospel, the figure of which is

[1] αἰῶνες αἰώνων.   [2] S. Matt. v. 18.

B

not in the law, nor anything in the law, the substance of which may not be found under the gospel;
God's once oppressed and captive Israel being the
vessel, in and by which He would shew out His purpose of grace and truth to other lost ones.

Observe, then, not only that the first-fruits are
gathered, some at the feast of the Passover, and
others not till Pentecost, while the " feast of tabernacles," or, as it is called, the " feast of ingathering,"
is not held until the seventh month, " in the end of
the year, when thou hast gathered in thy labours
out of the field;" [1] but how no less distinctly both
cleansing and redemption are ordained to take effect
at different times and seasons. I refer to those
mystic periods of " seven days,"[2] " seven weeks,"[3]
" seven months,"[4] " seven years,"[5] and the " seven
times seven years,"[6] which last complete the Jubilee,
which are all different times for cleansing and blessing men,—the former of which are figures of " the
ages," the last, of " the ages of ages," in the New
Testament; under which last blessed appointment
all those who had lost their inheritance, and could
not go free, as some did, at the Sabbatic year of rest,
might at length, after the " times of times," that is
the " seven times seven years," regain what had been
lost, and find full deliverance. For in the Sabbatic

[1] Exod. xxiii. 16 ; Lev. xxiii. 39 ; Deut. xvi. 13.
[2] Lev. xii. 2 ; xiii. 5, 21, 26 ; xiv. 8, &c.
[3] Lev. xxiii. 15.   [4] Lev. xvi. 29 ; xxiii. 24 ; Numb. xxix. 1.
[5] Lev. xxv. 4 ; Deut. xv. 9, 12.   [6] Lev. xxv. 8, 9.

year the release was for Israel only, not for foreign-
ers;[1] while in the Jubilee, liberty was to be proclaimed to all the inhabitants of the land.[2] What is
there in the ordinary gospel of this day, which in
the least explains or fulfils these various periods, in
and through which were wrought successive cleans-
ings and redemptions, not of persons only, but of
their lost inheritance? And if in the gospel, as now
preached, no truth is found corresponding with these
figures of the law, is it not a proof that something is
at least overlooked? God knows how much is overlooked from neglect of those Scriptures, which St.
Paul tells us are needed, "to make the man of God
perfect,"[3] but which by some are openly despised,
and by others are neglected, as the useless shadows
of a by-gone dispensation. In them is the key,
under a veil perhaps, of those "ages" and "ages of
ages," during which so many are debtors and bondsmen under judgment, without their true inheritance.
And though indeed it is true, that "it is not for us
to know the times and the seasons, which the Father
hath put in His own power,"[4] it is yet given us to
know that there are such times and seasons, and in
knowing it to gain still wider views of the "manifold
wisdom of God," and of the "unsearchable riches of
Christ," our Lord and Saviour.

It would far exceed my measure to attempt to
shew how the law in all its "times" figured the

---

[1] Deut. xv. 1, 3.   [2] Lev. xxv. 10.
[3] 2 Tim. iii. 16, 17.   [4] Acts i. 7.

E 2

gospel "ages." But I may give one more example
to prove, that in cleansing, as in giving deliverance,
God's method is to accomplish the end through appointed seasons, which vary according to a fixed rule,
—I refer to the different periods prescribed for the
purification of a woman on the birth of a male or of
a female child.[1] If a son is born, she is unclean in
the blood of her separation seven days, after which
she is in the blood of her purifying three and thirty
days, making in all forty days; but if she bear a
maid child, she is unclean for twice seven days, and
in the blood of her purifying six and sixty days, in all
eighty days; that is double the time she is unclean
for a man child. For the woman is our nature,
which if it receive seed, that is the word of truth,
may bring forth a son, that is "the new man;" in
which case nature, or the mother, which brings it
forth, is only unclean during the seven days of this
first creation, and then in the blood of purifying till
the end of the forty days, which always figure this
dispensation;[2] for wherever Christ is formed in us,
there is the hope that even "our vile body" shall
be cleansed, when we reach the end of this present

---

[1] Lev. xii. 1–5. A similar distinction of times is to be seen in
the cleansing of the leper; Lev. xiv. 7, 8, 9, 10, 20; and of those
who were unclean by the dead; Numb. xix. 12.

[2] The number "forty," wherever found in Scripture, always points
to the period of this dispensation, as the time of trial or temptation;
eg. Gen. vii. 1; Exod. xxiv. 18; Ezek. iv. 6; Deut. xxv. 2, 3;
S. Mark i. 13; Exod. xvi. 35; Numb. xiv. 33; 2 Sam. v. 4;
1 Kings xi. 42; Acts i. 3; and xiii. 21, &c.

dispensation. But if, instead of bearing this "new man," our nature only bear its like, a female child, that is fruits merely natural, then it is unclean for a double period, till twice seven days and twice forty pass over it. Here as elsewhere the veil will I fear hide from some what is yet revealed as to the varying times when cleansing may be looked for; but even the natural eye can see that two different times are here described; and those who receive this as the Word of God will perhaps believe that there is some teaching here, even if they cannot understand it. Those too, who believe that the Church was divinely guided in the order and appointment of the Christian Year, ought surely to consider what is involved in the fact that the purification of the woman after forty days is kept as one of the Church's holy days, under the title of "The Purification of St. Mary."[1] The Church of course reckons among her greatest days the conception and birth of that New and Anointed Man, who by almighty grace and power is brought forth out of our fallen human nature; but she does not forget to mark also the cleansing according to law, at the end of the mystic forty days, of that weak nature into which the Eternal Word has come, and out of which the New Man springs. There is like teaching in every time and season of the law, and its days and years figure the "ages" of the New Testament.

[1] Forty days after Christmas, that is on Feb. 2.

The prophets repeat the same teaching, still further opening out this part of God's purpose, in a later
age to visit those who are rejected in an earlier one,
and so to work through successive worlds or ages.
Thus though at the time they wrote Moab and Ammon were under a special curse, and cut off from the
congregation of Israel, according to the words, "Thou
shalt not seek their peace or prosperity for ever,"
and again, "Even to the tenth generation shall they
not enter into the congregation of the Lord for
ever;"[1] in obedience to which law both Ezra and
Nehemiah put away, not only the wives which some
Israelites had taken from these nations, but also the
children born of them;[2] though the prophets further declare the judgment of these nations, that
"Moab shall be destroyed,"[3] and "Ammon shall be
fuel for fire, and be no more remembered;"[4] yet they
declare also that "in the latter days the Lord shall
bring again the captivity of Moab and of the children
of Ammon."[5] Similar predictions are made respecting Egypt and Assyria,[6] Elam,[7] Sodom and her
daughters,[8] and other nations, who in the age of the

[1] Deut. xxiii. 3, 6. Heb. לְעוֹלָם; LXX., εἰς τὸν αἰῶνα.
[2] Ezra, x. 2, 3, 44; Neh. xiii. 1, 23, 25, 30
[3] Jer. xlviii. 42.   [4] Ezek. xxi. 28, 32.
[5] Jer. xlviii. 47, and xlix. 6.   [6] Isa. xix. 21, 25.
[7] Jer. xlix. 39.
[8] Ezek. xvi. 53, 55. Compare with this S. Jude 7, where we are
told that Sodom is "suffering the vengeance of eternal fire." (Gr.
πυρὸς αἰωνίου.) And yet of this very "Sodom and her daughters"
the prophet declares, that they shall "return to their former
estate."

prophets were " strangers to the covenants of promise, having no hope, and without God in the world," who yet are called to " rejoice with God's people," [1] and of whom even now an election, " though sometime far off, are made nigh by the blood of Christ." [2] These nations in the flesh were enemies, and as such received the doom of old Adam; yet for them also must there be hope in the new creation, according to the promise, " Behold, I make all things new." [3] For Christ, who, " being put to death in the flesh, but quickened in spirit, went in spirit and preached to the spirits in prison, which sometime were disobedient, when once the longsuffering of God waited in the days of Noah," [4] is " Jesus Christ, (that is Anointed Saviour,) the same yesterday, to-day, and for ever." [5]

Such is the light which the law and prophets give us as to God's purpose of salvation through successive ages. But even creation and regeneration, both works of the same God, tell no less clearly, though more secretly, the same mystery. God in each shews

[1] Deut. xxxii. 43 ; Rom. xv. 10. [2] Eph. ii. 12, 13.
[3] Rev. xxi. 5.
[4] 1 S. Peter iii. 18–20.
[5] Heb. xiii. 8. I may perhaps add here, that to me the scene recorded in S. Matt. viii. 28–34, and in the parallel passages of the other Evangelists, is most significant. Our Lord calls His disciples to "pass over to the other side," and there heals "the man possessed with devils, who had his dwelling among the tombs, exceeding fierce, whom no man could bind, no, not with chains." Christ not only heals all forms of disease in Israel, but casts out devils also on the other side of the deep waters.

how He works, not in one act, but by degrees,
through successive days or seasons. In creation each
day has its own work, to bring back some part of the
creature, and one part before another, from empti-
ness and confusion, to light and form and order. All
things do not appear at once. Much is unchanged,
even after "light" and a "heaven" are formed upon
the first and second days.[1] But these first works
act on all the rest, for by God's will this "heaven"
is a fellow-worker with God's Word in all the change
which follows, till the whole is "very good."[2] What
is this but the very truth of the first-born serving
the later-born? So in the process of our regeneration, there is a quickening, first of our spirits, then
of our bodies, the quickening of our spirits being
the pledge and earnest that the body also shall be
delivered in its season.[3] What a witness to God's
most blessed purpose; for our spirit is to our body
what the spiritual are to this world. And just as
the quickening of our spirit must in due time bring
about a quickening even of our dead and vile bodies;

[1] Gen. i. 4–8.

[2] The firmament was called "heaven," שָׁמַיִם, or "*the arrangers*,"
because it is an agent in arranging things on earth. "This appel-
lation was first given by God to the celestial fluid or air, when it
began to act in *disposing* or *arranging* the earth and waters. And
since that time the שָׁמַיִם have been the great agents in *disposing* all
material things in their places and orders, and thereby producing all
those wonderful effects which are attributed to them in Scripture, but
which it has been of late years the fashion to ascribe to *attraction,
gravitation*, &c."—Parkhurst, *sub voce*.

[3] Eph. i. 13, 14; Rom. viii. 11.

so surely shall the quickening and manifestation of
the sons of God end in saving those earthly souls
who are not here quickened. Thus does the microcosm foretell the fate of the macrocosm, even as the
macrocosm is full of lessons for the microcosm.

But even had we not this key, the language of
the New Testament, in its use of the word which our
Translators have rendered " for ever " and " for ever
and ever,"[1] but which is literally " for the age," or
" for the ages of ages," points not uncertainly to the
same solution of the great riddle, though as yet the
glad tidings of the " ages to come " have been but
little opened out. The epistles of St. Paul will prove
that the " ages " are periods, in which God is gradually working out a purpose of grace, which was ordained in Christ before the fall, and before those
" age-times,"[2] in and through which the fall is being
remedied. So we read, that " God's wisdom was ordained before the ages to our glory,"[3] that is, that
God had a purpose before the ages out of the very
fall to bring greater glory both to Himself and to His
fallen creature; then we are told distinctly of the
" purpose of the ages,"[4] shewing that the work of
renewal would only be accomplished through successive ages. Then we read, that " by the Son, God

---

[1] εἰς αἰῶνα, and εἰς αἰῶνας αἰώνων.

[2] χρόνοι αἰώνιοι.—2 Tim. i. 9 ; Tit. i. 2.

[3] 1 Cor. ii. 7 ; πρὸ τῶν αἰώνων.

[4] Eph. iii. 11 ; κατὰ πρόθεσιν τῶν αἰώνων ; translated, in our Authorized Version, " the eternal purpose."

made the ages,"[1] for it was by what the Eternal
Word uttered and revealed of God's mind in each
successive age that each such age became what it
distinctly was; each age, like each day of creation,
being different from another by the form and measure in which the Word of God was uttered or revealed in it, and therefore also by the work effected
in it, the work in each successive age, as in the different days of creation, being wrought first in one
measure, then in another, first in one part, then in
another, of the lapsed creation. Then again we read
of the " mystery which has been hidden from the
ages,"[2] and again that " the mystery," (for he repeats
the words,) " which hath been hid from ages and
generations, is now made manifest to the saints, to
whom God hath willed to make known what is the
riches of the glory of this mystery; which is, Christ
in you, the hope of glory."[3] In another place the
Apostle speaks of " glory to God in the church by
Christ Jesus, unto all generations of the age of
ages."[4] He further says, that Christ is set " far above
all principality, and power, and every name that is
named, not only in this age, but in the coming one;"[5]
and again, that " now once in the end of the ages He
hath appeared to put away sin by the sacrifice of
Himself;"[6] and that on us " the ends of the ages

[1] Heb. i. 2; and xi. 3.   [2] Eph. iii. 9.
[3] Col. i. 26.
[4] Eph. iii. 21; εἰς πάσας τὰς γενεὰς τοῦ αἰῶνος τῶν αἰώνων.
[5] Eph. i. 21.   [6] Heb. ix. 26; ἐπὶ συντελείᾳ τῶν αἰώνων.

are met;"[1] words which plainly speak of some of the ages as past, and seem to imply that other ages are approaching their consummation. Lastly, he speaks of "the ages to come," in which God will "shew the exceeding riches of His grace in His kindness towards us through Christ Jesus."[2]

Now what is this "purpose of the ages," which St. Paul speaks of, but of which the Church in these days seems to know, or at least says, next to nothing? I have already anticipated the answer. The "ages" are the fulfilment or substance of the "times and seasons" of the Sabbatic year and Jubilee under the old law. They are those "times of refreshment from the presence of the Lord, when He shall send Jesus Christ, who before was preached;"[3] and when, in due order, liberty and cleansing will be obtained by those who are now in bondage and unclean, and rest be gained by those who now are without their rightful inheritance. In the "ages," and in no other mystery of the gospel, do we find those "good things to come," of which the legal times and seasons were the "shadow."[4] Of course, as some of these "ages" are "to come,"

---

[1] 1 Cor. x. 11; τὰ τέλη τῶν αἰώνων κατήντησεν.

[2] Eph. ii. 4–7. I may add here that in all the following passages αἰὼν is used for this present or some other limited age or dispensation:—S. Matt. xii. 32; xiii. 39, 40; xxiv. 3; S. Luke xvi. 8; xx. 34, 35; Rom. xii. 2; 1 Cor. i. 20; ii. 6, 8; iii. 18; 2 Cor. iv. 4; Gal. i. 4; Eph. i. 21; ii. 2; vi. 12; 1 Tim. vi. 17; 2 Tim. iv. 10; Tit. ii. 12.

[3] Acts iii. 19.　　　　　[4] Heb. x. 1.

being indeed the "times and seasons which the Father hath put in His own power,"[1] we can as yet know little of their distinctive character, except that, as being the ages in which God is fulfilling His purpose in Christ, we may be assured their issue must be glorious. Yet they are constantly referred to in the New Testament, and the book of the Revelation more than any other speaks of them,[2] for this book opens out the processes and stages of the great redemption, which make up the Revelation of Jesus Christ which God gives Him; and this Revelation is not accomplished in one act, but through the "ages" and "ages of ages," foreshadowed by the "times" and "times of times" of the old law, the "age-times," again to use the language of St. Paul, in which the Lord is revealed as meeting the ruin of the creature. And the reason why we sometimes read of "ages," and sometimes of "the age," when both seem to refer to and speak of the same one great consummation, is, that the various "ages" are but the component parts of a still greater "age," as the seven Sabbatic years only made up one Jubilee. But because the mind of the Spirit is above them, men speak as if the varied and very unusual language of Scripture, as to the "ages" or the "age of ages," contained no special mystery. They will see one day that the subject is

---

[1] Acts i. 7.
[2] Rev. i. 6, 18; iv. 9. 10; v. 13, 14; vii. 12; x. 6; xi. 15; xiv. 11; xv. 7; xix. 3; xx. 10; xxii. 5.

dark, not because Scripture is silent, but only because men's eyes are holden.[1]

At any rate, and whatever the future "ages" may be, those past (and St. Paul speaks of "the ends" of some,) are clearly not endless; and the language of Scripture as to those to come seems to teach that they are limited, since Christ's mediatorial kingdom, which is "for the ages of ages," must yet be "delivered up to the Father, that God may be all in all."[2] And the fact that in John's vision, which describes the Revelation of Jesus Christ, which God gives Him, our Lord is called "Alpha and Omega, the beginning and the ending,"[3] seems to imply an end to the

---

[1] Every scholar knows that the expressions, εἰς τοὺς αἰῶνας, εἰς αἰῶνα αἰῶνος, εἰς αἰῶνα αἰώνων, εἰς τοὺς αἰῶνας τῶν αἰώνων, are unlike anything which occurs in the heathen Greek writers. The reason is, that the inspired writers, and they alone, understood the mystery and purpose of the "ages." They, or at least the Spirit which spake by them, saw that there would be a succession of "ages," a certain number of which constituted another greater "age." It seems to me that when they simply intended a duration of many "ages," they wrote εἰς τοὺς αἰῶνας, or "to the ages." When they had in view a greater and more comprehensive "age," including in it many other subordinate "ages," they wrote εἰς αἰῶνα αἰώνων, that is "to the age of ages." When they intended the longer "age" alone, without regard to its constituent parts, they wrote εἰς αἰῶνα αἰῶνος, that is "to an æonial age"; this form of expression being a Hebraism, exactly equivalent to εἰς αἰῶνα αἰώνιον: like "liberty of glory," for "glorious liberty," (Rom. viii. 21,) and "body of our vileness," for "our vile body." (Phil. iii. 21.) When they intended the several comprehensive "ages" collectively, they wrote εἰς τοὺς αἰῶνας τῶν αἰώνων, that is "to the ages of ages." Each varying form is used with a distinct purpose and meaning.

[2] Compare Rev. xi. 15, and 1 Cor. xv. 24.

[3] Rev. xxi. 6.

peculiar manifestation of Him as King and Priest, under which special offices the Revelation shews Him, offices which, as they involve lost ones to be saved and rebels ruled over, may not be needed when the lost are saved and reconciled. Would it not have been better therefore, and more respectful to the Word of God, had our Translators been content in every place to give the exact meaning of the words, which they render " for ever," or " for ever and ever," but which are simply " for the age," or " for the ages of ages;" and ought they not in other passages, where the form of expression in reference to these "ages" is marked and peculiar, to have adhered to the precise words of Holy Scripture? I have already referred to the passage of St. Paul, in his Epistle to the Ephesians, which in our Version is rendered " throughout all ages, world without end," but which is literally, " to all generations of the age of ages."[1] But even more remarkable are the words, in St. Peter's Second Epistle, which our Version translates " for ever," but which are literally " for the day of the age ;"[2] the key to which may perhaps be found in a preceding verse of the same chapter, where the Apostle says, that " one day is with the Lord as a thousand years, and a thousand years as one day."[3] These and other

---

[1] Eph. iii. 21.
[2] 2 S. Pet. iii. 18; εἰς ἡμέραν αἰῶνος, which, I may add here, is an exact literal translation of the words in Micah v. 2, מימי עולם, and which in our Authorized Version are translated " from everlasting."   [3] Verse 8.

similar forms of expression cannot have been used without a purpose. It is, therefore, matter of regret that our Translators should not have rendered them exactly and literally ; for surely the words which Divine Wisdom has chosen must have a reason, even where readers and translators lack the light to apprehend it.

The " ages," therefore, are periods in which God works, because there is evil and His rest is broken by it, but which have an end and pass away, when the work appointed to be done in them has been accomplished. The " ages," like the " days" of creation, speak of a prior fall : they are the " times" in which God works, because He cannot rest in sin and misery. His perfect rest is not in the " ages," but beyond them, when the mediatorial kingdom, which is " for the ages of ages,"[1] is " delivered up,"[2] and Christ, by whom all things are wrought in the ages, goes back to the glory which He had " before the age-times,"[3] "that God may be all in all."[4] The words " Jesus Christ, (that is, Anointed Saviour,) the same yesterday, to-day, and for the ages," imply that through these " ages" a Saviour is needed, and will be found, as much as " to-day" and "yester-

---

[1] Rev. xi. 15.   [2] 1 Cor. xv. 24.

[3] 2 Tim. i. 9; and Tit. i. 2 ; πρὸ χρόνων αἰωνίων; translated, in our Version, "before the world began." The Vulgate translation here is, " Ante sæcularia tempora," which is as literal a rendering as possible.

[4] 1 Cor. xv. 28.   [5] Heb. xiii. 8; εἰς τοὺς αἰῶνας.

day." It will I think too be found, that the adjective[1]
founded on this word, whether applied to "life,"
"punishment," "redemption," "covenant," "times,"
or even "God" Himself, is always connected with
remedial labour, and with the idea of "ages" as
periods in which God is working to meet and correct
some awful fall. Thus the "æonial covenant,"[2]
(I must coin a word, to shew what is the term used
in the original,) is that which comprehends "the
ages," during which "Jesus Christ is the same," that
is, a Saviour; an office only needed for the fallen,
for "they that are whole need not a physician." The
"æonial God," (language found but once in the New
Testament,[3]) refers, as the context shews, to God as

---

[1] *αἰώνιος.*   [2] Heb. xiii. 20.

[3] Rom. xvi. 25, 26. In this passage we read, first, of "the
mystery kept secret from *the æonial times,*" μυστήριον χρόνοις αἰωνίοις
σεσιγημένον, (translated in our English version, "Since the world
began,") and then of "*the æonial God,*" αἰωνίου Θεοῦ, "by whose
command this mystery is now made manifest." Is it not reasonable
to conclude that the same word, twice used here in the same sentence, must in each case have the same sense. But as applied to
"times," passing or past, *æonial* cannot mean *never-ending.* In the
Septuagint version of the Old Testament, the epithet *αἰώνιος* is only
applied to God four times, in one of which the corresponding עוֹלָם
of the Hebrew is not to be found; though in all the reference is
direct, either to "the age of ages," or to God's redeeming work as
wrought through "the ages." The passages are Gen. xxi. 33, where
after the birth of Isaac, the type of Christ, God is known by this
name אֵל עוֹלָם; then Isa. xxvi. 4, and xl. 28, in both which the
context shews the reason for the epithet; and lastly Job xxiii. 12,
in which passage the LXX. have given us *αἰώνιος* for אלהים or
Elohim, in the original; which name, as we see from a comparison
of Gen. i. and ii., (in the former of which God is always Elohim, in

working His secret of grace through " æonial times,"
that is, successive worlds or " ages," in some of
which " the mystery has been hid, but now is made
manifest by the commandment of the æonial God,"
that is, (if I err not,) the God who works through
these " ages." And so of the rest, whether " redemption,"[1] "salvation,"[2] "spirit,"[3] "fire,"[4] or "inheri
tance,"[5] all of which in certain texts are called "æonial,"
the epithet seems to refer to the same remedial plan,
wrought out by God through " worlds " or " ages."
And does not our Lord refer to this in the well-known
words, " This is life eternal,[6] (that is, the life of the
age or of the ages,) that they may know Thee, the
only true God, and Jesus Christ, whom Thou hast
sent "?[7] Does He not say here, that to know the only
true God, as the sender of His Son to be a Saviour,
and to know that Son as a Saviour and Redeemer,
mark and constitute the renewed life which is
peculiar to the ages? Æonial or eternal life therefore is not, as so many think, the living on and on for
ever and ever. It is rather, as our Lord defines it, a
life, the distinctive peculiarity of which is, that it has

the latter Jehovah Elohim,) refers to One who is working through
periods of labour to change a ruined world, until His image is seen
ruling it ; a title not lost when the day of rest is reached, but to
which another name, shewing what God is in Himself, is then added.
In Exod. iii. 15, we read of God's ὄνομα αἰώνιον, that is, His name as
connected with deliverance. I believe the word is never used but in
this connection. See further below, Note 1, page 66.

[1] Heb. ix. 12.   [2] Heb. v. 9.   [3] Heb. ix. 14.   [4] Jude 7.
[5] Heb. ix. 15.   [6] ἡ αἰώνιος ζωή.
[7] S. John xvii. 3.

F

to do with a Saviour, and so is part of a remedial plan.
This, as being our Lord's own explanation of the word,
is surely conclusive as to its meaning. But even had
we not this key, the word carries with it in itself its
own solution; for "æonial" is simply "of the ages;"
and the "ages," like the days of creation, as being
periods in which God works, witness, not only that
there is some fall to be remedied, but that God
through these days or ages is working to remedy it.[1]

---

[1] As to the Old Testament use of the word "age" or "ages," (translated "for ever" in the English Version,) a few words may be added
here. We have first the unconditional promise of God, that "the
seed of Abraham shall inherit the land for ever;" לְעוֹלָם; LXX.,
εἰς τὸν αἰῶνα; Exod. xxxii. 13. The same words are used of the
Aaronic priesthood; Exod. xl. 15; of the office of the Levites;
1 Chron. xv. 2; of the inheritance given to Caleb; Joshua xiv. 9;
of Ai being a desolation; Joshua viii. 28; of the leprosy of Gehazi
cleaving to his seed; 2 Kings v. 27; of the heathen bondsmen whom
Israel possessed, of whom it is said, "They shall be their bondsmen for ever;" Lev. xxv. 46. The same words are also used of the
curse to come on Israel for their disobedience:—"These curses shall
come on thee, and pursue thee till thou be destroyed; and they shall
be upon thee for a sign, and upon thy children for ever;" Deut.
xxviii. 45, 46. So of Ammon and Moab it is said:—"Thou shalt
not seek their peace for ever;" Deut. xxiii. 6; and again, "They
shall not come into the congregation of the Lord for ever;"
Deut. xxiii. 3; here עַד עוֹלָם. In all these and other similar instances, עוֹלָם and its equivalent αἰών mean the age or dispensation.
In Exod. xxi. 6. where the ear of the servant, who will not go free,
is bored, and he becomes a "servant for ever," (עוֹלָם; LXX., εἰς
τὸν αἰῶνα,) the sense must necessarily be much more limited; as
also in 1 Sam. i. 22. It is to be observed also that not only the
singular, עוֹלָם, as in 1 Kings ix. 3, and 2 Kings xxi. 7, but the
plural, עוֹלָמִים, is used in 1 Kings viii. 13, and 2 Chron. vi. 2, in
reference to the temple at Jerusalem. The double expression,
לְעוֹלָם וָעֶד, is variously translated by the LXX.; sometimes εἰς τὸν

Be this as it may, the adjective, " æonial" or age-
long, cannot carry a force or express a duration
greater than that of the ages or "æons" which it
speaks of. If therefore these "ages" are limited
periods, some of which are already past, while others,
we know not how many, are yet to come, the word
" æonial" cannot mean strictly never-ending. Nor
does this affect the true eternity of bliss of God's
elect, or of the redeemed who are brought back to
live in God, and to be partakers of Christ's " endless
life,"[1] of whom it is said, "Neither can they die

αἰῶνα καὶ ἔτι, as in Dan. xii. 3, where it is used of those " that turn
many to righteousness;" sometimes τὸν αἰῶνα καὶ ἐπ' αἰῶνος καὶ ἔτι,
as in Exod. xv. 18, where it is used of God; sometimes εἰς τὸν αἰῶνα
τοῦ αἰῶνος, as in Psalm xlv. 2, where it is used of Christ and His
kingdom; while in Micah iv. 7, the same Hebrew words, here
עולם וְעַד, are translated by the LXX., and here only, by the plural,
ἕως εἰς τοὺς αἰῶνας. More commonly, however, עַד עולם is rendered
simply ἕως τοῦ αἰῶνος by the LXX., as in Gen. xiii. 15, Joshua
iv. 7, and elsewhere. Lastly, in Dan. vii. 18, we have both the
singular and the plural form together, עַד עָלְמָא וְעַד עָלַם עָלְמַיָּא,
rendered by the LXX., ἕως αἰῶνος τῶν αἰώνων.

The adjective αἰώνιος is used continually by the LXX.,—in refer
ence to the Passover, Exod. xii. 14, 17,—the tabernacle service,
Exod. xxvii. 21,—the priestly office of the sons of Aaron, Exod.
xxviii. 43,—the meat-offering, Lev. vi. 18,—and other things of the
Jewish dispensation, all of which are called νόμιμον αἰώνιον. So in
Jer. xxiii. 40, we have αἰώνιον ὀνείδεισμον, and ἀτιμίαν αἰώνιον, used
of the corrective judgments on Israel, whose restoration is also fore-
told. I will only add that the very remarkable language of S. Paul,
(2 Cor. iv. 17,) καθ' ὑπερβολὴν εἰς ὑπερβολὴν αἰώνιον, seems intended
to add to the force of the word αἰώνιος, which could scarcely be, if
αἰώνιος meant *eternal.* Beza's comment here is, " æternitas ipsâ
æternitate magis æterna." See too Corn. a Lapide, *in loco.*

[1] See Heb. vii. 16. The word here used of Christ's resurrection-
life, which we share with Him, is ἀκατάλυτος, translated in our

any more, for they are equal to the angels, and are
the children of God, being the children of the resurrection ;"[1] for this depends on a participation in the
divine nature, and upon that power which can "change
these vile bodies, that they may be fashioned like
unto Christ's glorious body, according to the working
whereby He is able to subdue even all things unto
Himself."[2]

(3) It yet remains to shew that this purpose of
God, wrought by Him through successive worlds or
ages, is only accomplished through death and dissolution, which in His wisdom He makes the means
and way to life and higher glory ; for it is " by death,"
and by death only, that He " destroys him that has
the power of death, that is the devil, and delivers
them who through fear of death were all their lifetime subject to bondage."[3] Nature everywhere reveals
this law, though the divine chemistry is often too
subtle to allow us to see all the stages of the trans-
formations and the passages or " pass-overs" from life
to death and death to life, which are going on around
us everywhere.   But the great instance cited by
our Lord, that " except a corn of wheat fall into the
ground and die, it abideth alone, but if it die, it

Version *" endless"* ; literally *" indissoluble"* ; a word never used in
Scripture respecting judgment or punishment, but only of that life
which is beyond all dissolution.

[1] S. Luke xx. 36.

[2] Phil. iii. 21. See also 1 Cor. xv. 53; Rom. viii. 29; Heb. vii.
16; xii. 28; 1 S. Pet. i. 3, 4, 5; 1 S. John iii. 2.

[3] Heb. ii. 15.

brings forth much fruit,"[1] forces the blindest to confess that all advance of life is through change, and death, and dissolution. The seed of the kingdom, which is above all kingdoms, and the seed of the Son, who is above all sons, does not, any more than the seed of wheat or the seed of man, come to perfection in a moment or without many intermediate changes, but "goes from strength to strength,"[2] from the bursting of one shell of life to fuller life, from the opening of one seal to another, and "from glory to glory,"[3] till all is perfected. Christ has shewn us all the way, from "the lowest parts of the earth,"[4] from the Virgin's womb, through birth, and infant swaddling clothes, to opened heavens, through temptation, and strong crying and tears, and the cross, and grave, and resurrection, and ascension, till He sits down at God's right hand to judge all things. And the elect yield themselves to the same great law of progress through death, and "faint not though the outward man perish, that their inward man may be renewed day by day."[5] Others may think they will be saved in another way than that Christ trod. His living members know it is impossible. To them, as the Apostle says, "to live is Christ;"[6] and they cannot live His life without being "partakers of His sufferings."[7] Therefore "we which live are alway

---

[1] S. John xii. 24.
[2] Psalm lxxxiv. 7.
[3] 2 Cor. iii. 18.
[4] Psalm cxxxix. 15.
[5] 2 Cor. iv. 16.
[6] Phil. i. 21.
[7] 2 Cor. i. 5; Phil. iii. 10; Col. i. 24.

delivered unto death for Jesus' sake, that the life
also of Jesus might be made manifest in our mortal
flesh."[1]   Because this is so little seen,—because so
many take or mistake Christ's cross as a reprieve to
nature, rather than a pledge that nature and sin
must be judged and die, seeming to think that
Christ died that they should not die, and that their
calling is to be delivered *from* death, instead of *by*
it and *out of* it ;[2]—because in a word the meaning of
Christ's cross is not understood, but rather perverted,
and therefore death is shrunk from, instead of being
welcomed as the appointed means by which alone
we can be delivered from him that has the power of
death, who more or less rules us till we are dead, for
" sin reigns unto death,"[3] and only " he that is dead
is freed from sin ;"[4]—because this, which is indeed
the gospel, is not received, or if received in word is
not really understood, even Christians misunderstand
what is said of that destruction and judgment, which
is the only way for delivering fallen creatures from
their bondage, and bringing them back in God's life
to His kingdom.

As this is a point of all importance, lying at the
very root of the cross of Christ and of His members,
and giving the clue to all the judgments of Him, who

[1] 2 Cor. iv. 11.

[2] Our translators have sometimes rendered ἐκ θανάτου by the
English words "*from* death ; " as in Heb. v. 7 ; but the force of the
original is always "*out of* death."

[3] Rom. v. 21.   [4] Rom. vi. 7.

"killeth and maketh alive," who " bringeth down to the grave and bringeth up,"[1] I would shew, not the fact and truth only, that for fallen creatures the way of life is and must be through death, but also the reason for it, why it must be thus, and cannot be otherwise. For the cross is not a fact or truth only, but power and wisdom also, even God's power and wisdom;[2] as power, meeting the craving of our hearts for deliverance; as wisdom, answering every question which our understanding can ask as to the mystery of this life. For both to head and heart life is indeed a riddle, which neither the Greek nor Jew, the head and heart of old humanity, could ever fully solve, though each people by its special craving shewed its wants; the Jew, as St. Paul says, requiring signs of power, for the heart wants and must have something to lean upon; the Greek, man's head or mind, seeking after wisdom, for it felt the darkness and asked for some enlightening. To both God's answer was the cross of Christ, which gave to each, to head and heart, what each was longing for; power to the one to escape from that which had tied and bound it, for by death with Christ we are freed from the bondage of corruption and from all that hinders the heart's best aspirations; wisdom to the other to see why we must die, and what is the reason for all present suffering.

As to the fact and doctrine, a few words may

---

[1] 1 Sam. ii. 6; Deut. xxxii. 39.   [2] 1 Cor. i. 18-24.

suffice, for in one form or another it is the creed of
all Christendom, that for fallen man the way of life
is and only can be through death and judgment.
The cross the way to life—this is confessedly the
special teaching of the gospel. But what is the
cross? Does Christ's death save us unless by grace
we die with Him? Our Lord distinctly says, "If any
man will come after me, let him deny himself, and
take up his cross, and follow me; for whosoever will
save his life shall lose it; and whosoever will lose his
life for my sake shall find it."[1] "This is a faithful
saying, If we be dead with Him, we shall live with
Him: if we deny Him, He also will deny us."[2] The
saint must say, "I am crucified with Christ, nevertheless I live, yet not I, but Christ liveth in me."[3]
"We are debtors, not to live after the flesh, for if we
live after the flesh we shall die; but if we through
the Spirit do mortify the deeds of the body, we shall
live."[4] In baptism therefore we profess our death
with Christ, that dying with Him we may also live
with Him.[5]

Such is the doctrine we all receive. But what
is the reason for it? Why is the way of life for us
through the cross, that is through death? Why
cannot it be otherwise? If we see the way by which
man got away from God, we shall see the way of
his return, and why this must be through death; for

[1] S. Matthew xvi. 25.   [2] 2 Tim. ii. 11, 12.
[3] Gal. ii. 20.   [4] Rom. viii. 12 13.
[5] Rom. vi. 3, 4.

indeed the way, by which we came away from God, must be retraced if by grace we come back to Him.

How then did man depart from God, and die to Him, and fall from His kingdom ? By believing a lie. By the serpent's double lie,—a lie about God, that God grudges and is not true, and a lie about man, that in disobedience he shall be as God,—the divine life in man's soul was poisoned and destroyed, and man was separated from God, and died to God's world.[1] And because to a being like man, made in God's image, death cannot be the end of existence, but is only a passing out of one world into another, by this death to God man who is a spirit lost the place which God had given him, the Paradise, called by Paul " the third heaven,"[2] and was driven out, and fell into the kingdom of darkness, his inward life turned like sweet wine to sourest vinegar, into a life of ceaseless aching restlessness ; to escape which he turns to outward things, hating to come to himself even for a moment, unconsciously driven by his own inward dissatisfaction to seek diversion from himself in any outward care, pleasure, or vanity ; while his body became like that of the beasts, subject to the elements of this world, and to all the change and toil which make up " the course of this world."

Such was the fall of man, and it explains why death is needful for our return to God. Death is the

[1] Gen. iii. 1–5.

[2] 2 Cor. xii. 2, 4. Paradise is the word used by the LXX. in Gen. ii. 8, 9. Compare Rev. ii. 7.

only way out of any world in which we are. It was
by death to God we fell out of God's world. And it is
by death with Christ to sin and to this world that we
are delivered in spirit from sin, that is the dark world,
and in body from the toil and changes of this outward
world.   For we are, as Scripture and our own hearts
tell us, not only in body in this outward world, but
in our spirits are living in a spiritual world, which
surely is not heaven, for no soul of man till regenerate is at rest or satisfied ; and being thus fallen, the
only way out of these worlds is death : so long as we
live their life, we must be in them.   To get out of
them, therefore, we must die : die to this elemental
nature, to get out of the seen world, and die to sin,
to get out of the dark world, called in Scripture "the
power of darkness."[1]   And since the life of the one
is toil and change, and the life of the other is dissatisfaction and inward restlessness, we must die to both
if we would be free from the changes of this world,
and from the restlessness and dissatisfaction in which
by nature our spirits are.   Christ died this double
death for us, not only " to sin,"[2] but also " to the
elements of this world."[3]   And to be free, we also
must die with Him to both.   Only by such a death
are we delivered.

In pressing this point however, that death is needful for the sinner's deliverance, I need scarcely add,
that death, alone, and without another life, is not and

[1] Col. i. 13.   [2] Rom. vi. 10.   [3] Col. ii. 20.

cannot of itself be enough to bring us back to God's world. We need death to get out of this world and out of the power of darkness; but we also need and must have the life of God, which is only perfected in resurrection, to live in God's world.[1] Just as without the life of this world, we could not enter this world, or without the life of hell, enter or live in hell; so without the life of heaven we cannot enter or live there; for we cannot live in any world without the life of it. And therefore as the serpent's lie kindled the life of hell in man, before he could fall into the power of darkness, so God's life must be quickened again in man, before he can live again in God's kingdom. And, blessed be God, as the life of hell was quickened by a lie, so the life of God is quickened by the truth, even by the Word of God, who came where man was to raise up God's life in man, in and by which through a death to sin and to this world man might be freed perfectly.[2] In Christ the work has been accomplished. In Him by God's Word and Spirit God's life has been again raised up in man; and in the power of this life man in Christ has died both to sin and to the world, and so, through death, resurrection, and ascension, by steps we yet know little

[1] S. John iii. 3, 5.
[2] Not without a deep and wondrous reason is בשׂר both *Good-news* and *Flesh* in the Hebrew; for by the one as by the other the captive creature is reached and quickened. Great indeed is the mystery of the flesh of Christ, touching which there are indeed many unspeakable words, which it is not lawful for a man to utter. Yet the mystery is revealed from faith to faith.

of, has come back out of darkness to God's right hand.
Through Christ the self-same work is yet accomplish-
ing, to bring lost man by the same process to the same
blessedness.   But whether in Christ, or in us, the
work is only wrought through death.   Man to be
saved must not only be quickened by God's life, but
must also die to that which keeps him far from God.
And the way to bring about this death is God's
judgment, who, because He loves us, kills to make
alive, and "turneth man to destruction," that He
may say, "Return, ye children of men."[1]

And this explains why God alone of all teachers
has had two methods, and must have them, namely,
law and gospel, which appear opposed, for law condemns while the gospel justifies, each to meet one
part of our need and of the devil's double lie.   For
man is yet held by both parts of this old lie, that God
grudges and is untrue, and that man by self-will may
be as God ; and he needs not only to have God's life
quickened again in him, whereby he may be prepared
to live in God's world, but no less to have the life of
hell and of this world slain in him, by which he may
be delivered out of that power of darkness and of
this present world, which hold him captive, that so
he may come back again to God's kingdom.   To
meet the first, we have the promise or gospel, long
before the law, though only fulfilled after law has
done its work ; to meet the second, we have the law

---

[1] Psa. xc. 3.   See also Job xix. 10, and ix. 22.

which condemns, and proves that man is not as God,
but a fallen, ruined creature. By the one, God's life
is quickened in man; by the other, through present
or future judgment, the hellish and earthly life is
slain and overcome. Does not God love? The
gospel is the answer. Is man as God? The law
settles this. Christ's cross is the seal of both, revealing that God is love, for He gives His Son for rebels;
and that man is not as God, but a sinner under death
and judgment.

But while the law condemns and shews what man
is, this " ministry of condemnation," needful in its
place, is not and cannot be God's end. The gospel,
the " ministration of righteousness and life," is God's
proper work, and, therefore, as St. Paul says, " remaineth;"[1] but the law, the " ministration of death
and condemnation," God's " strange work,"[2] is only
a means to the end, and therefore " to be abolished "
and " done away."[3] St. Paul's teaching on this point
is most express, though spite of his teaching, and spite
of the gospel, not a few even of the Israel of God
cannot yet steadfastly look to the end of that which
is abolished. No less clear also is his witness as to
God's promise to Abraham's seed, that it is not and
cannot be altered or disannulled by the law, or by
that curse and wrath and judgment which the law
worketh.[4] So in his Epistle to the Galatians, having

[1] 2 Cor. iii. 11.   [2] Isa. xxviii. 21.
[3] 2 Cor. iii. 11, 13.
[4] Rom. iv. 15; v. 20; vii. 9, 11; Gal. iii. 10, 19.

first shewn that God's promise to Abraham included
all nations, and that the law necessarily could only
bring judgment, he proceeds to argue that " this covenant of promise which was confirmed before of God
in Christ, the law, which was four hundred and thirty
years after, cannot disannul, that it should make the
promise of none effect; for if the inheritance be of
the law, it is no more of promise; but God gave it
to Abraham by promise."[1]   The law, which is and
must be judgment to men, is needed to slay and
overthrow them in their own eyes. But this killing
is to make alive. The judgment or condemnation
cannot in any case disannul the previous covenant.
"Though it be but a man's covenant, yet if it be
confirmed, no man disannulleth or addeth thereto."
Judgment therefore must issue in blessing, not blessing in judgment. But for most the veil is yet on
Moses' face, so that in looking at the " ministry of
condemnation" men cannot see " the end of the
Lord," and that the Lord is very pitiful and of tender
mercy.[2]

I have dwelt the more on this, because so few now
seem to see why for us the way of life is and must
be through death ; and because, if this be seen, God's
end and purpose and the reason of His judgments
will be more evident. God our Father judges to
save. He only saves by judging what is evil. The
evil must be overthrown; and through death God

·   [1] Gal. iii. 8, 15, 17, 18.
      [2] 2 Cor. iii. 13 ; S. James v. 11.

destroys him that has the power of death. A new
creation, which is only brought in through death, is
God's remedy for that which through a fall is held in
death and bondage. Therefore both the "earth and
heavens" must "perish and be changed."[1] Therefore God Himself "turns us to destruction" that we
may "return" as little children.[2] And God's elect
accept this judgment here, that their carnal mind
may die, and the old man be slain with all his en-
mity. The world reject God's judgment here, and
therefore have to meet it in a more awful form in the
resurrection of judgment in the coming world. For
while here, through the burdens and infirmities of
"this vile body,"[3] our fallen spirit is more easily
broken, and we die to sin more quickly; though even
here we need both fires and waters, to make us die to
that self-willed life which is our misery. Who can
tell how much harder this death may be to those, who,
having gone hence, have not the burden of "this
vile body" to humble the pride of that fallen spirit,
which, while unbroken, is hell, and which must die
in us if we would reach God's rest.

Such is the reason for salvation by the cross, that
is through death; but the great illustration here
as elsewhere is to be found in the law, that appointed
"shadow of good things,"[4] which in all its varied
forms of sacrifice asserts the same great truth, that
only by the fire of God and through death can the

---

[1] Heb. i. 10–12.
[2] Psa. xc. 3.
[3] Phil. iii. 21 ; τὸ σῶμα τῆς ταπεινώσεως.
[4] Heb. x. 1.

earthly creature be changed, and so ascend to God.
The offerings were indeed of different kinds, some of
a sweet savour, which were offered on the altar in
the tabernacle;[1] while others not of a sweet savour
were burnt on the earth, in some place outside the.
camp of Israel;[2] figuring the varied relations in
which men's works and persons might stand to God,
and the varying place and manner of their acceptance by Him. But in either case, whether offered in
obedience voluntarily, or required penally for trespass
and disobedience, the offering ever was made by fire,
and so perished in its first form to rise in another,
as pillars of smoke before God. If then all this was
"the pattern of things in the heavens,"[3] we have
another witness that a transformation wrought by
fire is yet being carried on in the true heavens, that
is the spiritual world. For no divine change can be
wrought even on God's elect, save by "passing
through the waters and through the fires" which are
appointed for us, waters and fires as real, though not
of this world, as those which burnt on the altar of
old, or moved in the laver of the tabernacle. Our
Lord can no more spare our nature than the animal
was spared of old by the priest who offered it. And
as He in His own body, made under the law, did
not shrink from, but fulfilled, the types of suffering,
so will He fulfil the same in the bodies of those who
are His members, that "being made conformable

[1] Lev. i. ii. iii.
[2] Lev. iv. v. vi.   [3] Exod. xxv. 40; Heb. ix.,23.

unto His death, they may attain unto the resurrec
tion from among the dead."[1]

In any case the way for all is through the fires,
for fire is the great uniter and reconciler of all
things ; and things which without fire can never be
united, in and through the fire are changed and
become one. Therefore every coming of Christ, even
in grace, is a day of judgment. Therefore there are
fires even for the elect both now,[2] and in the coming
day ;[3] for "our God is a consuming fire ;"[4] and to
dwell in Him we must have a life, which, because it
is of the fire, for fire burns not fire, can stand unhurt
in it. Therefore our Lord " came to cast fire into
the earth," and desired nothing more than " that it
should be already kindled ;"[5] therefore He says,
" Every one shall be salted with fire, and every
sacrifice shall be salted with salt."[6] For this is the
very " baptism of the Holy Ghost and fire,"[7] that
" spirit of judgment and of burning," promised by
the prophet, " with which the Lord shall purge away
the filth of the daughters of Zion, and cleanse the
blood of Jerusalem ; after which He will create on
every dwelling place of Mount Zion, and on all her
assemblies, a cloud of smoke by day, and the brightness of a flame of fire by night ; and upon all, the
glory shall be a defence ;"[8] for " He is like a refiner's

---

[1] Phil. iii. 10, 11.

[2] 1 S. Pet. i. 7, and iv. 12.

[3] 1 Cor. iii. 13, 15.

[4] Heb. xii. 29.

[5] S. Luke xii. 49.

[6] S. Mark ix. 49.

[7] S. Matt. iii. 11.

[8] Isa. iv. 4, 5.

G

fire, and like to fuller's soap; and He shall sit as a
refiner and purifier of silver, and He shall purify
the sons of Levi as gold and silver are purged,
that they may offer to the Lord an offering of
righteousness."[1]   And as by the hidden fire of this
present life, shut up in these bodies of corruption, we
are able by the wondrous chemistry of nature through
corruption to change the fruits and flesh of the earth
into our blood, and from blood again into our flesh
and bone and sinew; so by the fire of God can we
be changed, and made partakers of Christ's flesh and
blood.   In and through Christ we have received this
transmutation;[2] and through His Spirit, which is
fire, is this same change accomplished in us.[3]

---

[1] Mal. iii. 3. Luther's well-known words are to the purpose here,
for though originally written by him as a test of prophets, they are
no less true in their measure of all who are taught of God:—
"Quærendum num experti sunt spirituales illas angustias, et nativi-
tates divinas, mortesque, infernosque. Si audieris blanda, tranquilla,
devota, (ut vocant,) et religiosa, etiamsi in tertium cœlum sese
raptos dicant, non approbabis. Quia signum Filii Hominis deest, qui
est Basanos, probator unicus Christianorum, et certus spirituum
discretor. Vis scire locum, tempus, modum, colloquiorum divinorum.
Audi :—' Sicut leo contrivit ossa mea,' et 'Projectus sum a facie
oculorum tuorum :' ' Repleta est malis anima mea, et vita mea
inferno appropinquavit.' Tenta ergo, et ne Jesum quidem audias
gloriosum, ni videris prius crucifixum."—*Epist.* lib. ii. p. 42.

[2] Rom. v. 11 ; τὴν καταλλαγήν.

[3] It is surely a significant fact, that the two words, תמם and
כלה, used in Hebrew to express *destruction*, signify also, and are
used to express, *perfection* ; and that the word for *a sacrifice by fire,*
אשה, is the same as that for a *bride* or *wife*; e.g. Numb. xxviii. 6.
By this double sense a veil covers the letter, veiling yet revealing
God's purpose; for His purpose to the creature is through *destruction*

And as with the first-fruits, so with the harvest.
The world to be saved must some day know the same
baptism. For "the Lord will come with fire," and "by
fire and by His sword will He plead with all flesh,
and the slain of the Lord shall be many."[1] The
promised baptism or outpouring of the Spirit must
be judgment, for the Spirit cannot be poured on man
without consuming his flesh to quicken a better
life;[2] and "His sword, which cometh out of His
mouth,"[3] is that Word, which kills to make alive
again. God is indeed "a man of war;"[4] but His
warfare and wrath, unlike the "wrath of man, which
worketh not the righteousness of God,"[5] works both
righteousness and life, and is set forth in that "warfare of the service of the tabernacle,"[6] by which that
which was of the earth was made to ascend to God
through fire a sweet sacrifice.

The view therefore which has been accepted by
some believers, as more in accordance with Scripture

to *perfect* it, and by *fire* to make it a *bride* unto the Lord. For a
kindred reason some of the angels are called Seraphim, that is
burning ones; for like the Lord, whose throne is flames of fire, (Dan.
vii. 9, 10,) they also are as fire; as it is written, "He maketh His
angels spirits, His messengers a flame of fire." Heb. i. 7, and Psalm
civ. 4.

  [1] Isa. lxvi. 15, 16.

  [2] Isa. xl. 7 ; and compare Rev. viii. 6, 7, which describes the
effect produced by the breath or spirit of the Lord sounding through
the trumpets of the heavenly sanctuary.

  [3] Rev. xix. 13, 15.   [4] Exod. xv. 3.   [5] S. James i. 20.

  [6] See Numbers iv. 23, 30, &c., and viii. 24, 25 ; margin : and
compare 1 Tim. i. 18.

than the popular notion of never-ending torments,
that those who abuse their day of grace will, after suffering more or fewer stripes, according to the measure of their transgressions, be utterly annihilated by
the " second death,"[1] though a great step in advance
of the doctrine of endless woe, is not a perfect witness of the mind of God, nor the true solution of the
great mystery.   God has not made man to let him
fall almost as soon as made, and then, in a large proportion of his seed, to sin yet more, and suffer, and
be annihilated ; but rather out of and through the
fall to raise him even to higher and more secure
blessedness ; as it is written, " As in Adam all die,
so in Christ shall all be made alive ;"[2] not all at
once, but through successive ages, and according to
an appointed order, in which the last even as the
first shall be restored by the elect ; for Christ is not
only the " First," but also " with the last,"[3] and will
surely in the salvation of " the last " bring into view
some of His glories, not inferior to those which are
manifested in the salvation of " the first-born," who
are " His body."[4] He is the " First," both out of life
and out of death,[5] and as such He manifests a peculiar glory in His elect first-born. But He is also the
" Last,"[6] and " with the last," and as such He will

[1] I refer to the view advocated in such works as *Eternal Punishment and Eternal Death*, by the Rev. J. W. Barlow ; and *Endless
Sufferings not the Doctrine of Scripture*, by the Rev. T. Davis.

[2] 1 Cor. xv. 22.   [3] Isa. xli. 4.   [4] Eph. i. 23.
[5] Col. i. 15, 18.   [6] Isa. xliv. 7 ; Rev. i. 11, 17.

display yet other treasures hid in Him, for "in Him are hid all treasures,"[1] and "riches unsearchable,"[2] which He will bring to light in due season. Their own conversion ought to give believers hopes of this. But indeed the whole mystery of regeneration and conversion, and the absolute needs-be for the cross, in its true ground and deep reason, is so little seen even by converted souls,—so ignorant are they, that, as first-fruits, they are called, not only to be "fellow-workers with God,"[3] but to be a pledge and pattern of the world's salvation,—that they misunderstand the plainest words which are spoken as to God's dealings in judgment with those who miss the glory of the first-born. For what is conversion but a passage, first through waters, then through fires;[4] a change involving a "death unto sin and a new birth unto righteousness;" the death not annihilating the fallen spirit, but rather being the appointed means for bringing forth and perfecting the new life. And though the harvest may, and does, need a greater heat than the first-fruits,—the one being gathered in autumn, in the seventh,[5]—the other in spring, in the first and third months,[6]—there is but one way to bring forth seed out of the earth, and but one means of ripening that which is so brought forth. Nothing is done without the waters and the fires. Conversion is only wrought through condemnation. The law

---

[1] Col. ii. 3.
[2] Eph. iii. 8.
[3] 1 Cor. iii. 9; 2 Cor. vi. 1.
[4] Isa. xliii. 2; S. Matt. iii. 11.
[5] Lev. xxiii. 39.
[6] Lev. xxiii. 6, 10, 12, 16, 17.

condemns and slays us,[1] not to annihilate, but to
bring forth a better life. And those souls, who do not
know this condemnation, never fully know the "justification of life"[2] in resurrection. Why then should
the judgment of the " second death," which is the
working of the same ministry of condemnation on the
non-elect, be annihilation? Will not the judgment,
because God changes not, in them, as in the elect,
be the means of their deliverance? To me all Scripture gives but one answer; that there is but one way;
" one baptism for the remission of sins ; " that " baptism wherewith we have to be baptized," and of which
we may each say with our Head, " How am I strait-
ened until it be accomplished ; "[3] that " burning
in us, which," St. Peter teaches, " is made to prove
us," and at which we should " rejoice, inasmuch as we
are thus partakers of Christ's sufferings ; "[4] that
" therefore we are buried by baptism into death ; "[5]
and therefore we look to be " baptized with the Holy
Ghost and fire ; "[6] not surely to annihilate, but rather
through judgment to perfect us; and that, therefore, and to the same end, those not so baptized here
must know the last judgment, and " the lake of fire,
which is the second death."[7] And indeed if one
thinks of the language of the true elect, and of all
the " fiery trial " which they are called to pass
through,—when we hear them say, or say ourselves,

---

[1] Rom. vii. 9-11.   [2] Rom. v. 18.   [3] S. Luke xii. 50.
[4] 1 S. Pet. iv. 12—τῇ ἐν ὑμῖν πυρώσει, κ.τ.λ.
[5] Rom. vi. 4.   [6] S. Matt. iii. 11.   [7] Rev. xxi. 8.

" Thou hast laid me in the lowest pit, in darkness, in the deeps; thy wrath lieth hard upon me, and Thou hast afflicted me with all thy waves,"[1]—we shall not so easily misunderstand what is said of that judgment, which is required to melt the greater hardness and impenitence of the reprobate.[2]

It is therefore simply because God is what He is, that He is, though love, and because He is love, the curse and destruction of the impenitent. But as even in this fallen world He is able, not only to turn our blessings into a curse,[3] but curses into blessings ;—as we see strength, and health, and wealth, and talents, which are blessings, all turned to curses through disobedience; and pain, and want, and sorrow, and death, which are curses, turned to real blessings ;—so in other worlds, because God changes not, curses by Him may yet be turned to blessings; and they who now are turning blessings into a curse may, and, I believe, will, find that God can make even curses blessings. Paul's words should help us here. He who could say, " To me to live is Christ,"[4] and whose ways were therefore a true expression of God's mind, bids the Church " to deliver some to Satan, for the destruction of their flesh and saving of their spirit,"[5] and further tells us that he himself has done this, and " delivered" certain brethren "to Satan, that they may learn not to blaspheme."[6]   Oh wondrous

[1] Psa. lxxxviii. 6, 7.   [2] See Appendix, Note A. p. 169.
[3] Mal. ii. 2.   [4] Phil. i. 21.
[5] 1 Cor. v. 5.   [6] 1 Tim. i. 20.

ways of God! Souls are taught not to blaspheme, by
being delivered to Satan; and the spirits of Christian
brethren are saved, and their flesh destroyed, by
being put into the hands of God's adversary.   What
does this not teach us as to God's purpose towards
those whom He also delivers to Satan, and disciplines
by evil, since they will not learn by good.   "Whoso
is wise and will observe these things, even they shall
understand the loving-kindness of the Lord." [1]

I cannot even attempt here to trace the stages or
processes of the future judgment of those who are
raised up to condemnation; for if "the righteousness of God is like the great mountains, His judgments are a great deep; [2] but what has here been
gathered from the Word of God, as to the course
and method of His salvation, throws great light on
that "resurrection of judgment," [3] which our Lord
speaks of.   Of the details of this resurrection, of the
nature and state of the bodies of the judged,—if indeed bodies in which there is any image of a man,
and therefore of God, (for man's form bears God's
image, [4]) then are given to them,—and of the scene
of the judgment,—very little is said in Scripture;
but the peculiar awfulness of the little that is said
shews that there must be something very fearful in
it.   And indeed, when one thinks of the eternal law,
"To every seed its own body," [5] one can understand
how terrible must be the judgment on all that grows

[1] Psa. cvii. 43.   [2] Psa. xxxvi. 6.   [3] S. John v. 29.
[4] 1 Cor. xi. 7.   [5] 1 Cor. xv. 38.

in a future world from the seed which has been nourished here of self-love and unbelief; a judgment in comparison with which any present pain is light affliction. It is thus described:—"And I saw a great white throne, and Him that sat on it, from whose face the earth and the heaven fled away; and there was found no place for them. And I saw the dead, small and great, stand before God; and the books were opened; and another book was opened, which is the book of life: and the dead were judged out of those things which were written in the books, according to their works. And the sea gave up the dead which were in it; and death and hell delivered up the dead which were in them; and they were judged every man according to their works. And death and hell were cast into the lake of fire. This is the second death."[1] And yet, awful as it is, who can doubt the end and purpose of this judgment, for "God, the judge of all,"[2] "changes not,"[3] and "Jesus Christ" is still "the same, yesterday, to-day, and for the ages."[4] And the very context of the passage, which describes the casting of the wicked into the lake of fire, seems to shew that this resurrection of judgment and the second death are both parts of the same redeeming plan, which necessarily involves judgment on those who will not judge themselves, and have not accepted the loving judgments and sufferings, which in this life prepare the first-

[1] Rev. xx. 11–14.   [2] Heb. xii. 23.
[3] Mal. iii. 6.   [4] Heb. xiii. 8.

born for the first resurrection. So we read, —" And He that sat upon the throne said, Behold, I make all things new. And He said unto me, Write : for these words are true and faithful. And He said unto me, It is done. I am Alpha and Omega, the beginning and the end. I will give to him that is athirst of the fountain of the water of life freely. He that overcometh shall inherit all things ; and I will be his God, and he shall be my son. But the fearful, and unbelieving, and the abominable, and murderers, and whoremongers, and sorcerers, and idolaters, and all liars, shall have their part in the lake which burneth with fire and brimstone ; which is the second death."[1] What does He say here but that " all things shall be made new," though in the way to this the fearful and unbelieving must pass the lake of fire. And does not the fact that the threatened judgment comes under, and is part of, the promise, " I make all things new," shew that the second death is not outside of or unconnected with it, but is rather the appointed means to bring it about in some cases. Those who overcome inherit all: they are God's sons and heirs. Like Abraham, they are " heirs of the world ;"[2] " the world is theirs,"[3] to bless it. But the judgment of the wicked, even the second death, is only the conclusion of the same promise, which, under threatened wrath, as in the curse of old upon

[1] Rev. xxi. 5–8.   [2] Rom. iv. 13.   [3] 1 Cor. iii. 22.

the serpent, involves the pledge of true blessing. What but this could make Paul, who so yearned over his brethren that he " wished himself accursed for them," " have hope," not fear, " that there should be a resurrection of the dead, both of the just and unjust." [2]

The " second death "[3] therefore, so far from being, as some think, the hopeless shutting up of man for ever in the curse of disobedience, will, if I err not, be God's way to free those who in no other way than by such a death can be delivered out of the dark world, whose life they live in. The saints have died with Christ, not only " to the elements of this world,"[4] but also "to sin,"[5] that is, the dark spirit-world. By the first they are freed from the bondage of sense ; by the second, from the bondage of sin, in all its forms of wrath, pride, envy, and selfishness. The ungodly have not so died to sin. At the death of the body therefore, and still more when they are raised to judgment, because their spirit yet lives, they are still within the limits of that dark and fiery world, the life of which has been and is the life of their spirit. To get out of this world there is but one way, death ; not the first, for that is passed, but the

---

[1] Gen. iii. 14–19. " How mysterious are God's ways. . . Neither to Adam nor to Eve was there one word of comfort spoken. The only hint of such a thing was given in the act of cursing the serpent. The curse involved the blessing."—*The Eternal Purpose of God*, by A. L. Newton, p. 10.

[2] Compare Rom. ix. 3, and Acts xxiv. 15. [3] Rev. xx. 14.
[4] Col. ii. 20 [5] Rom. vi. 10.

second death. Even if we have not light to see this, ought not the present to teach us something as to God's future ways; for is He not the same yesterday, to-day, and for ever? We know that, in inflicting present death, His purpose is through death to destroy him that has the power of death, that is the devil. How can we conclude from this, that, in inflicting the second death, the unchanging God will act on a principle entirely different from that which now actuates Him? And why should it be thought a thing incredible that God should raise the dead, who for their sin suffer the penalty of the second death? Does this death exceed the power of Christ to overcome it? Or shall the greater foe still triumph, while the less, the first death, is surely overcome? Who has taught us thus to limit the meaning of the words, " Death is swallowed up in victory "? Is God's " will to save all men "¹ limited to fourscore years, or changed by that event which we call death, but which we are distinctly told is His appointed means for our deliverance? All analogy based on God's past ways leads but to one answer. But when in addition to this we have the most distinct promise, that " as in Adam all die, so in Christ shall all be made alive,"—that " death shall be destroyed,"—that " there shall be no more curse," but " all things made new," and " the restitution of all things; "—when we are further told that " Jesus Christ is the same,"

¹ 1 Tim. ii. 4.

that is a Saviour, "yesterday, to-day, and for the ages;"—the veil must be thick indeed upon man's heart, if spite of such statements "the end of the Lord" is yet hidden from us.

To me too the precepts which God has given are in their way as strong a witness as His direct promises. Hear the law respecting bondmen,[1] and strangers,[2] and debtors,[3] and widows and orphans,[4] and the punishment of the wicked, which may not exceed forty stripes, "lest if it exceed, then thy brother should seem vile unto thee;"[5] yea even the law respecting "asses fallen into a pit:"[6]—hear the prophets exhorting to "break every yoke," to "let the oppressed go free," and to "undo the heavy burdens:"[7]—hear the still clearer witness of the gospel, "not to let the sun go down upon our wrath,"[8] to "forgive not until seven times, but until seventy times seven,"[9] "not to be overcome of evil, but to overcome evil with good:"[10] to "walk in love as Christ has loved us," and to "be imitators of God as dear children:"[11]—see the judgment of those who neglect the poor, and the naked, and the hungry, and the stranger, and the prisoner;[12]—and then say, Shall God do that which He abhors? Shall He command that bondmen and debtors be freed, and

---

[1] Deut. xv. 12-15.
[2] Exod. xxii. 21 ; Lev. xix. 33, 34.
[3] Deut. xv. 1, 2, 9.
[4] Exod. xxii. 22 ; Deut. xxiv. 17.
[5] Deut. xxv. 2, 3.
[6] Exod. xxi. 33, 34; and xxiii. 4, 5.
[7] Isa. lviii. 6
[8] Eph. iv. 26.
[9] S. Matt. xviii. 22.
[10] Rom. xii. 21.
[11] μιμηταὶ Θεοῦ, Eph. v. 1, 2.
[12] S. Matt. xxv. 41-43.

yet Himself keep those who are in worse bondage
and under a greater debt in endless imprisonment?
Shall He bid us care for widows and orphans, and
Himself forget this widowed nature, which has lost
its Head and Lord, and those poor orphan souls which
cannot cry, Abba, Father? Shall He limit punishment to forty stripes, "lest thy brother seem vile,"
and Himself inflict far more upon those who though
fallen still are His children? Is not Christ the
faithful Israelite, who fulfils the law; and shall He
break it in any one of these particulars? Shall He
say, "Forgive till seventy times seven," and Himself
not forgive except in this short life? Shall He command us to "overcome evil with good," and Himself,
the Almighty, be overcome of evil? Shall He judge
those who leave the captives unvisited, and Himself
leave captives in a worse prison for ever unvisited?
Does He not again and again appeal to our own
natural feelings of mercy, as witnessing "how much
more" we may expect a larger mercy from our
"Father which is in heaven"?[1]   If it were otherwise, might not the adversary reproach, and say,
Thou that teachest and judgest another, teachest
Thou not thyself? Not thus will God be justified.
But, blessed be His Name, He shall in all be justified.
And when in His day He opens "the treasures of
the hail,"[2] and shews what sweet waters He can bring

[1] S. Matt. vii. 6-11; and compare Psa. ciii. 8-14.
[2] Job xxxviii. 22. The two questions of the book of Job are,
How can man, and How can God, be justified? Job's complainings,

out of hard hailstones; when He unlocks "the place where light now dwells" shut up, and reveals what light is hid in darkness and hardness, as we see in coal and flint, those silent witnesses of the dark hard hearts, which God can turn to floods of light; when we have "taken darkness to the bound thereof,"[1] and have seen not only how "the earth is full of God's riches," but how He has "laid up the depths in storehouses;"[2] in that day when "the mystery of God is finished," and He has "destroyed them which corrupt the earth,"[3]—then shall it be seen how truly God's judgments are love, and that "in very faithfulness He hath afflicted us."[4]

§ III. *Popular Objections.*

I have thus stated what I see of God's purpose and way; and it is, I believe, the key to all the difficulties and apparent contradictions of Holy Scripture on this subject. There are, however, certain current objections, which have weight with those

in substance, amount to this,—How can God be justified in treating me as He does? His three friends, who cannot answer this, urge him rather to ask, How can man be justified? Elihu answers this latter question; and God then answers Job's question by asking him if he knows what God can bring out of things which at present are dark and crooked. Job's question is not the sinner's question, but that of the "perfect man;" (ch. i. 8.) a question not unacceptable to God, who declares of Job's three friends, that "they have not spoken of me the thing which is right, like my servant Job." ch. xlii. 8.

[1] Job xxxviii. 19, 20.   [2] Psa. civ. 24; and xxxiii. 7.
[3] Rev. xi. 18.   [4] Psa. cxix. 75.

who tremble at God's Word. It is said that this doctrine is opposed to the voice of the Church, to Reason, and above all to Holy Scripture. If this last be true, the doctrine cannot stand. God's Word is the final appeal on this and every other subject. For the rest, if the Church speak with God, woe to those who disobey her. But if by reasonings or traditions she make void the Word of God, " let God be true, and every man a liar." [1]

Let us look at these objections :—

(1) First, it is said that the Church has never held, but on the contrary has distinctly condemned, this doctrine. But is this true? Where then, I ask, and when, has the Catholic Church ever authoritatively condemned this view of restitution? At what council, or in what decrees, received by East and West, shall we find the record and the terms of this condemnation? Of course I am aware that individuals have judged the doctrine, and that since Augustine's days the Western Church, led by his great authority, has generally received his view of endless punishment. I know too that Theophilus of Alexandria, the persecutor of Chrysostom, [2] and then Anastasius of Rome, who, according to his own confession, until called upon to judge Origen, knew little or nothing about him, [3] and later on the bishops at the " home synod " summoned by the patriarch Mennas

---

[1] Rom. iii. 4.
[2] For details, see Neander, *Church Hist.* vol. iv. pp. 474–476.
[3] Id. *ibid.* p. 472.

at Constantinople, the latter acting under court influence, two hundred years after his death, condemned Origen.[1] But so have certain bishops in
council asserted Transubstantiation, and condemned
all those who on this point differed from them; and
yet it would be most untrue to say that the Universal Church asserted this doctrine, or that a rejection of it involved a rejection of the Christian faith.
It is so with the doctrine of endless torments. It
can never be classed under "Quod semper, quod
ubique, quod ab omnibus." Many have held it; but
the Catholic Church has nowhere asserted it; while
not a few of the greatest of the Greek Fathers distinctly dissent from it.[2] The Creeds received by East
and West at least know nothing of such a doctrine,
and in their assertion of "the forgiveness and remission of sins," seem rather to point to another belief
altogether.

But suppose it were otherwise,—suppose it could
be shewn that the Church, instead of asserting "the
forgiveness of sins," had taught the reverse, and had

[1] Both Neander and Gieseler shew, that this condemnation of
Origen was passed, not at the 5th General Council of Constantinople, in 553, as some have supposed, but at the "home synod"
under Mennas, in 541. See Neander, *Church Hist.* vol. iv. p. 265;
and Gieseler, *Eccl. Hist.* Second Period, div. ii. ch. 2, § 109; and
notes 8 and 20. And even this "home synod," though under court
influence it condemned some of Origen's views, would not consent
to condemn the doctrine of Restitution, spite of the Emperor's
express requirement that this doctrine should be anathematized.

[2] See *Appendix*, Note B., pp. 174—190, for extracts from
Clement of Alexandria, Gregory of Nazianzus, Gregory of Nyssa,
and many others.

H

judged the doctrine of restitution,—grant further, what I admit, that the Church generally has seen, or at least has taught, comparatively little, especially of late, respecting universal restoration,—what does this prove, if, though yet beyond the Church's light, the doctrine is really taught in Holy Scripture? Many things have been hid in Scripture for ages. St. Paul speaks of " the revelation of the mystery, which had been hid from ages and generations; "[1] some part of which at least, though hidden, had been " spoken by the mouth of all God's holy prophets since the world began." [2] There are many such treasures hidden in Scripture, open secrets like those in nature which are daily opening to us. But when have God's people as a body ever seen or received any truth beyond their dispensation? Take as an instance Israel of old, whose ways, " ensamples of us,"[3] prefigure the Church of this age. Did they ever receive the call of the Gentiles, or see God's purpose of love outside their own election? A few all through that age spoke of blessings to the world, and were without exception judged for such a testimony :—" Which of the prophets have not your fathers slain?" Was God's purpose to the Gentiles therefore a false doctrine : or, because His people did not receive it, was it not to be found in their own Scriptures? The doctrine of " the restitution of all things " is to the Church what " the

[1] Rom. xvi. 25, 26 ; Eph. iii. 5.   [2] Acts iii. 21.
[3] 1 Cor. x. 6; τύποι ἡμῶν.

call of the Gentiles" was to Israel. And if the
Church, like Israel, can see no truth beyond its own,
and has judged those who have been witnesses to a
purpose of love far wider than that of this age,—
which is not to convert the world, as some suppose,
but only "to take out of the nations a people for
God's name,"[1]—is God's purpose, though declared
in Scripture, to be damned as false doctrine, simply
because the Church is blind to it? Is Israel's path
to teach us nothing? Are men's traditions as to
God's purpose to be preferred to His own unerring
Word? When I see the Church's blindness at this
day, almost unconscious of the judgment which is
coming on it,—when I see that if I bow to the
decisions of its widest branch, I must receive not
Transubstantiation only, but the Immaculate Conception also,—the last of which cuts away the whole
ground of our redemption, for if the flesh which
bore Christ was not ours, His Incarnation does not
profit us,—I can only fall back on that Word, which
in prospect of coming apostasy is commended to
the man of God, as the guide of his steps and the
means to perfect him.[2] It is indeed a solemn thing
to differ with the Church, or like Paul to find one-
self in a "way which they call heresy," simply by
"believing," not some but, "all the things which

---

[1] Acts xv. 14. Compare S. Matt. xxiv. 14 :—"This gospel shall
be preached in all the world *for a witness* to all nations."

[2] 2 Tim. iii. 14–17. Compare the connexion of this passage with
the opening words of the chapter.

are written in the law and in the prophets."[1]   But
the path is not a new one for the sons of God.   All
the prophets perished in Jerusalem.[2]   And, above
all, the Lord of prophets was judged as a Deceiver,[3]
by those whom God had called to be His witnesses.
The Church's judgment, therefore, cannot decide a
point like this, if that judgment be in opposition
to the Word of God.

But is it possible that Christians should have
been allowed to err on so important a point as the
doctrine of future judgment? Would our Lord Himself have used, or permitted others to use, words
which, if final restitution be true, might be understood as teaching the very opposite? I say again,
look at the doctrine of Transubstantiation. Has,
or has not, one large section of the Church been
suffered to err as to the meaning of words, which
are at the very foundation of her highest act of
worship? Did not our Lord, when He said, "Take,
eat, this is my body,"[4] know how monstrously the
words would be perverted? Yet though a single
sentence would have made any mistake almost impossible, He did not add another word. Why?
Because the very form in which the Word is given
is part of our discipline ; and because without His
Spirit, let His words be what they may, we never
really understand Him. Transubstantiation is a
mistake built on Christ's very words ; and the doc-

[1] Acts xxiv. 14.   [2] S. Luke xiii. 33, 34.
[3] S. Matt. xxvii. 63.   [4] S. Matt. xxvi. 26.

trine of endless torments is but another like misunderstanding; which not only directly contradicts many other Scriptures, but practically denies and falsifies the glorious revelation of Himself, which God has given us in the gospel, and in the face of Jesus Christ. Both shew the Church's state. And though thousands of God's children have held, not these only, but many other errors, the fact, instead of approving their errors, only proves the grace of Him, who spite of such errors can yet bless and make His children a blessing.

(2) It is further said that the doctrine is opposed to Reason. Several arguments are urged by those whose opinions are entitled to the most respectful attention. I confess I care little to answer these, because to me the question simply is, "What saith the Scripture;" because, too, I know that those who urge these reasons would instantly abandon them, if they believed Scripture spoke differently; for I am sure I may answer for them and say, that no reasons if opposed to Scripture would weigh with them; because, too, if it be made a question of reasoning, as much may be said against as for the doctrine of never-ending punishment. Still, as some of these reasons are perplexing simple hearts, I may notice those which are most often heard.

(i) The first is, that this doctrine militates against the atonement, for if all men shall at length be saved, God became man to redeem from that which is equally remedied without it. Surely, Christ did not die to save us from nothing. But never will any believe the redemption by Christ, who do not believe in hell also.[1]

Now what does it say for the state of the Church, when men can argue, that if all are saved at last by Christ, they are saved as well without redemption. The objection only proves the confusion of thought which passes current for sound doctrine, and how little the nature of the fall, and the redemption by Christ, are really understood. What the Scripture teaches is, that man by disobedience and a death to God fell from God under the power of death and darkness, where by nature he is for ever lost, as unable to quicken his soul as to raise again his dead body; that in this fall God pitied man, and sent His Son, in whom is life, to be a man in the place where man was shut up, there to raise up again God's life in man, to bear man's curse, and then through death to bring man back in God's life to God's right hand; that in His own person, Christ, the first of all the first-fruits, as man in the life of God, broke through the gates of death and hell; that those who receive Him now through Him obtain the life by which they also shall rise as firstfruits of His creatures; that " if the firstfruits be holy, the lump is also holy," and that therefore "in Christ shall all be made alive." But how does it follow hence that those who are not firstfruits, if saved at all, are saved without Christ's

[1] Pusey's Sermon on *Everlasting Punishment*, p. 29; and Cazenove's Essay on *Universalism*, p. 13.

redemption? Christ is and must be the one and only way, by which any have been, or are, or can be, saved. But if when we were "dead in sins" and "children of wrath, even as others," God's Word could quicken and deliver us out of the horrible pit, that we might be "firstfruits of His creatures," why should we say He cannot bring back others out of death, though they miss the glory of being "firstfruits?" To say that if this be true, God became man to redeem us from what is equally remedied without it, and that if "in Christ all are made alive," their life is not through Christ's atonement, but independent of it, is simply misapprehension of the whole question. But the objection shews how much, or how little, is understood even by masters of Israel.

The other part of the objection, that "none believe in redemption who do not believe in hell," is true, and shews why some at least are only saved by being "delivered to Satan." For none are saved till they know or believe their ruin. Like the Prodigal, we must come to ourselves before we come to our Father.[1] If therefore yet bound by the lie, "Ye shall be as Gods," men will not believe their fall, and that there is, and that their souls are in, a dark world, the necessary result is they cannot believe in redemption, for till they believe their fall they will neither believe nor care for deliverance. If they will not believe it, they shall know it. And if belief in hell

---

[1] S. Luke xv. 17, 20.

makes belief in redemption possible, what if the knowledge of hell should also lead those, who will not believe, to the knowledge of their state and of their need of Christ's redemption?

(ii) It is further argued, that, if grace does not, judgment cannot, save man. How can damnation perfect those whom salvation has not helped? Can hell do more for us than heaven? What more could God do for us, that He has not done for us?[1]

The answer to this lies simply in what has been said above, as to the reason why the way of life for us must be through judgment. We are held captive by a lie. One part of that lie is that we are as Gods. The remedy for this is to shew us that we are ruined creatures. Till we believe or know this, we cannot return to God. Judgment, therefore, to shew us what we are, is as needful as the grace which meets the other part of the serpent's lie, and shews what God is. Therefore God kills to make alive. Therefore He turns man to destruction, that He may say, Return, ye children of men. Therefore He delivers even Christians to Satan, for the destruction of their flesh, that so they may learn what grace has not taught them. If we want further examples, Nebuchadnezzar shews us how judgment does for man what goodness cannot. Loaded with gifts, through self-conceit he loses his understanding. The remedy is to make him as a beast. Then as a beast he learns

[1] Pusey's Sermon, pp. 9, 10.

what as a man he had not learnt.[1] Let the nature
of the fall be seen, and the reason why we are only
saved through judgment is at once manifest. Grace
saves none but those who are condemned; nor till we
have felt "the ministry of death and condemnation"
do we fully know "the ministry of life and righteousness." The firstfruits from Christ to us are proofs,
that by death, and thus alone, is our salvation perfected. Unbelievers, who will not die with Christ,
are lost, because they are not judged here. God
cannot do more than He has done for man. Law
and Gospel are His two covenants. But why may not
the Lord, seeing that He is "Jesus Christ, the same
yesterday, to-day, and for the ages," by the ministry
of death and condemnation in another world do for
those, who have not here received it, that same work
of judgment to salvation, which in the firstfruits is
accomplished in this present world ? Blessed be His
name, we know He will subdue all things unto Himself; and though our sin can turn His blessings into
curses, He can no less turn curses into blessings, by
that same power which through death destroys the
power of death.

(iii) But it is further objected, that this doctrine
gives up God's justice;[2] for if all are saved, there
will be no difference between St. Peter and Nero,
virgins and harlots, saints and sinners.[3]

[1] Dan. iv. 29-34.   [2] Cazenove's Essay, pp. 22-24.
[3] Jerome, on Jonah iii. 6, 7 ; quoted from Huet's *Origeniana*, in
Pusey's Sermon, p. 29.

This again is misapprehension or worse. God's justice is given up, because He saves by judgment. The conclusion is absurd; but it arises from the common notion, that we are saved by Christ *from* death, instead of *by* it and *out of* it. What Scripture teaches is, that man is saved through death; that the elect, being first quickened by the word, and then judging themselves or being judged in this world,[1] by a death to sin are freed from Satan; that others, not so dying to sin, remain in the life and therefore under the curse and power of the dark world, and are therefore delivered to Satan to be punished, to know, since they will not believe, their fall, and their need of God's salvation. But all this simply asserts the justice of God, that if men will not be judged here, they must be in the coming world.

For the rest, the statement that according to this view no distinction is made between St. Peter and Nero, virgins and harlots, saints and sinners, is not only untrue,—for is there no distinction between reigning with Christ and being cast out and shut up in hell with Satan?—but is too like the murmur of the Elder Son at his brother's return,[2] to need any answer with those who know their own hearts. It is the old objection of the Pharisee and Jew, who thought God's truth would fail if sinners of the Gentiles shared their good things; an objection deeply rooted in the natural heart, which is slow to believe that an outwardly pure and blameless life needs as

[1] 1 Cor. xi. 31, 32.   [2] S. Luke xv. 29, 30.

much the blood of the cross as the most depraved and open sinner. The objection only shews where they are who urge it; and whatever support it may seem to have from a part of God's Word,—as a part of God's Word, taken against the rest, seemed to justify the Jew, and was indeed the very ground on which he rejected the call of the Gentiles,—more light will shew that it rests on partial views, and on a systematic disregard of all those truths of Scripture, which are beyond the dispensation. Some day we shall see, that "all have come short,"[1] that as to sin and failure "there is no difference between the Jew and Greek,"[2] that the elect are "by nature children of wrath, even as others,"[3] that if saved at all, first or last we must be "saved by grace;"[4] and this truth will justify all God's ways, "who hath concluded all in unbelief, that He might have mercy upon all."[5]

(iv) The last argument I notice is that from analogy. It is said that as unnumbered creatures in this world fail to attain their proper end, as a large proportion of seeds never germinate, as many buds never blossom or reach perfection, so thousands of our race may also miss their true end, and be for ever castaways. "For as the husbandman soweth much seed upon the ground, and planteth many trees, and yet the thing that is sown good in his season cometh not up, neither doth all that is planted take root; even

---

[1] Rom. iii. 23.   [2] Rom. x. 12.   [3] Eph. ii. 3.
[4] Eph. ii, 8.   [5] Rom. xi. 32.

so it is of all them that are sown in the world; they shall not all be saved." [1]

Now that countless creatures in their present form fail to reach that perfection, which some of their species reach, and which seems the proper end of it, is a fact beyond all contradiction. Present nature is both the witness and mirror of man's present state. But to say that nature out of this failure or destruction cannot and does not bring forth other and often fairer forms of life,—that what here fails of its due end is therefore wholly lost, or for ever shut up in the imperfect form in which it dies and fails here,— is opposed to fact and all philosophy. While therefore it may be fairly argued that many of our race fail to attain that perfection which is reached by some as the end of this present life, analogy will never prove that those who miss this are hopelessly destroyed, or for ever held in the ruined form or state which they have fallen into. If this indeed were the conclusion to be drawn from the failure of some seeds, why not go further and argue that since death overcomes every form of life in this world, death and not life must be the final ruler of the universe? A sad and most partial reading this of the great mystery. The truth is, nature is a mirror of the two unseen worlds. Every form of death, all disease, decay, and failure, every fruitless seed, each ruined life, is the shadow of hell, and of the working of that spirit

[1] 2 Esdras viii. 41.

which destroys and mars God's handiwork. On the
other hand all life and joy, every birth, all that
quickens and supports and helps the creature, is a
reflection of the world of light, and a witness that
God is meeting the disorder. Even death itself, as
seen in nature, does not declare annihilation or never-
ending bondage in any given form of evil. Quite the
reverse. Nature says, matter cannot perish : it may
seem to perish, but the apparent death is only change
of form; the change, call it death or what you will,
being indeed the witness of present imperfection, but
not of eternal bondage in that form, nor of destruction or annihilation when that form perishes. Nature
must be strangely read to draw this lesson from it ;
but in this argument the conclusion depends upon the
extent or limit of our view, and our capacity to read
the book of nature, imperfect readings of which will
always lead us, as in the phenomena of sunrise and
sunset, to conclusions the very opposite to reality.
Analogy, so far from proving that the lost are for
ever shut up in the form of evil where they now are
or may be, declares not only that all things may be
changed, but that what to sense appears destroyed
and worthless, may contain shut up in itself what is
most beauteous and valuable. Think of the precious
things which chemistry brings out of refuse,—of the
flavours, scents, and colours, which are every day
being extracted from what appears worthless. Who
can tell what may yet be wrought by fire ? Fire
can free and transform what water cannot touch.

All things shall be dissolved by fire.[1] And even those most fair and least corruptible, as the precious stones, which are the shadows of the things of Christ's kingdom,[2] shall, like that kingdom, one day give up their present beauty for a higher glory, that God may be all in all.

(v) The greatest difficulty perhaps of all is that which meets us from the existence of present evil. "The real riddle of existence," says an acute thinker, "the problem which confounds all philosophy, aye, and all religion too, so far as religion is a thing of man's reason, is the fact that evil exists at all; not that it exists for a longer or a shorter duration. Is not God infinitely wise and holy and powerful now? And does not sin exist along with that infinite holiness and wisdom and power? Is God to become more holy, more wise, more powerful, hereafter; and must evil be annihilated to make room for His perfections to expand?"[3] No doubt the existence of evil is a difficulty; but surely this kind of reasoning about it proves too much; for by the same reasoning it might be shewn, that God could never have done anything. Was He not "infinitely wise and holy and powerful" when "the earth was without form and void"? Why then should this state ever have been changed by Him till "all was very good"? Why should not the darkness, which once reigned, have remained for ever? Was the

---

[1] 2 S. Peter iii. 12.   [2] Exod. xxviii. 17–21; Rev. xxi. 19–21

[3] Mansel's *Bampton Lectures*, lect. vii. p. 222.

change needed " to make room for God's perfections
to expand"? And why, when the earth was again
corrupt, should God judge it with a flood ; and then
again bring it forth from its destruction? Why
should He work for the deliverance of His people in
Egypt, or " triumph gloriously" over their oppressors?
Was He not " all wise, all holy, and all powerful,"
even while His people were oppressed? Did He become " more holy and wise and powerful " by their
deliverance? If such reasoning as this is good, why
should we look either for a day of judgment or the
promised times of restitution? Why, but because,
mysterious as the fact is, there has been a fall. All
things do not continue as they were from the beginning. And therefore the Father "worketh hitherto,"[1]
nor rests till " all things are made new,"[2] and " everything is very good."

And as to evil, granting that its existence is a
difficulty, is it one which is so utterly incomprehen-
sible? Is it not plain that the knowledge of evil is
essential to the knowledge and experience of some
of the highest forms of good ; and cannot even man's
reason see that sin may be a means of bringing
even into heaven a meekness and self-distrust and
knowledge of God, which could be gained in no other
way? Does not all nature shew that while the origin
of evil is unspeakable, death and corruption may
both be means to bring in better things? The seed

---

[1] S. John v. 17.   [2] 2 Cor. v. 17 ; Rev. xxi. 5.

falls into the ground, and dies, and becomes rotten;
but the result is a resurrection with large increase.
So the juice of grapes or corn is put into the still,
and thence by decomposition and fermentation, both
forms of corruption, is evolved a higher and more
enduring purity and spirituality. The existence of
evil therefore is not so much the difficulty, as the
question, whether, if evil be essential now, it may
not be always needful for the same end. And to this
question our reason as yet can give no answer. Scripture however has an answer, that, though a fall has
been permitted, evil shall have an end, and the creature through God's wondrous wisdom even by its
fall be raised to higher glory. Scripture distinctly
teaches that "the creature was made subject to
vanity, not by its own will, but through Him who
subjected the same in hope ; because the creature
itself also shall be delivered from the bondage of
corruption into the glorious liberty of the children
of God."[1] What St. Paul says too of an election of
grace before the foundation of the world, according
to a predetermined purpose of redemption through
Christ's precious blood,[2] proves that God's purpose
involved and could only be wrought out through a
fall, for without a fall there can be no redemption.
And the fact that God, with the full foreknowledge
of man's sin, chose yet to encounter all this sin, with
its attendant misery, out of it to bring forth and give

<hr/>

[1] Rom. viii. 20, 21.   [2] Eph. i. 4–12.

to man His own righteousness, shews that in His judgment it was worth while to suffer the evil in order to arrive at the appointed end. Evil therefore must subserve some good purpose—otherwise God could never permit it, or say, "I form peace, and I create evil." [1] And though as yet we cannot fully see why evil is allowed, what we know of God and of His ways, that there is perfect wisdom and economy in every part of them, assures us that there can be no error or mistake, even in that which seems to cause the ruin of the creature. Meanwhile those who believe that some now bound by death by it are being brought into more perfect and secure blessedness, by such a creed practically assert that present evil need not be eternal, since in some at least it shall be done away. If in some, why not in all? Besides, even supposing we could not tell whether evil might or might not be done away,—supposing it were proved that it would exist for ever, as essential to the training of certain creatures,— this existence of evil for ever would be a very different thing from the idea of the infinite or never-ending punishment of a finite being. But, thank God, we are not left to guesses. Prophecy announces a day when there shall be no more curse or death, but all things made new. In this witness we may rest, spite of the fact and mystery of present evil.

(vi) I have thus noticed what Reason is supposed

[1] Isa. xlv. 7.

I

to say against the doctrine of final restitution.   But
to me this is a question only to be settled by the
Word of God ; for with our knowledge or lack of
knowledge of all the mystery of our being, we are
not in a position to argue this point, or to say exactly
what is, or what is not, reasonable.   What saith the
Scripture ?   This is the question, and the only question I care to ask here on this subject.   At the same
time I confess that the restitution of all things, so
far from appearing to me unlikely or unreasonable,
seems, spite of the mystery of the origin and existence of evil, more consistent with what we know of
God than the doctrine of never-ending punishment.
To say that sin, assuming it to be opposed to God,
has the power of creating a world antagonistic to
God as everlasting as He is, attributes to it a power
equal at least to His ; since, according to this view,
souls whom God willed to be saved, and for whom
Christ died, are held in bondage under the power of
sin for ever ; and all this in opposition to the Word
of God, which says that God's Son "was manifested
that He might destroy the works of the devil,"[1] who,
if the so called orthodox view be right, will succeed
in destroying some of the works of the Son of God
for ever.

When I think too of God's justice, which it is
said inflicts, not only millions of years of pain for
each thought or word or act of sin during this short

[1] 1 S. John, iii. 8.

life of seventy years,—not even millions of ages
only for every such act, but a punishment which
when millions of ages of judgment have been inflicted for every moment man has lived on earth is
no nearer its end than when it first commenced;
and all this for twenty, forty, or seventy years of sin
in a world which is itself a vale of sorrow;—when I
think of this, and then of man, his nature, his weakness, all the circumstances of his brief sojourn and
trial in this world; with temptations without, and a
foolish heart within; with his judgment weak, his
passions strong, his conscience judging, not helping
him; with a tempter always near, with this world to
hide a better;—when I remember that this creature,
though fallen, was once God's child, and that God is
not just only, but loving and long-suffering;—I cannot say my reason would conclude, that this creature,
failing to avail itself of the mercy here offered by
a Saviour, shall therefore find no mercy any more,
but be for ever punished with never-ending torments.

Natural conscience, which with all its failings is
a witness for God, protests against any such awful
misrepresentation of Him. For even nature teaches
that all increase of power lays its possessor under an
obligation to act more generously. Shall not then
the Judge of all the earth do right?[1] Shall we say
that sinful men are selfish and guilty, if with wealth

[1] Gen. xviii. 25.

and power they neglect the poor and miserable; and yet that God, who is eternal love, shall do what even sinful men abhor and reprobate? For shall we, if one of our children fall and hurt itself, or be lost to us for years, bitterly reproach ourselves for want of care, and be tormented with the thought that with greater watchfulness we might have saved the child,—shall we if at last he is found, even among thieves, a sharer of their crimes, still love him as our own child, make every possible excuse for him, and do all we can to save him,—shall we, though he be condemned, plead for him to the end, urging the strength of those temptations with which he has been so long surrounded,—and shall not God have at least the like pity for His lost ones? Has He left any of His children in peril of being for ever stolen from Him? Can He, if through the seduction of a crafty tempter some wander for awhile, be content that they should remain miserable slaves for ever lost to Him? He would not be a wise man who risked even an estate, nor a good man who obliged any one else to do so. Can God then ever have exposed His children to the risk of endless separation from Him? All the reason God has given me says, God could not act thus; and that if His children are for ever lost, He even more than they must be miserable. But, as I have said, we have, thank God, a better guide than our reason, even God's blessed Word, with its "more sure" promise; and because that Word declares man's final restitution, and that God

will seek His lost ones "till He find them,"[1] and
that therefore a day shall come when "there shall
be no more curse or death," I gladly accept God's
testimony, and look for life and rest, spite of present
death and judgment and destruction.

(3) But it is said, certain texts of Holy Scripture
are directly opposed to the doctrine of universal
restitution. That they seem opposed is granted. We
have already seen that, taken in the letter, text clashes
with text on this subject. All those texts which speak
of "destruction" and "judgment" are explained by
what has been said above as to the way of our salvation, and that by death alone God destroys him
that has the power of death. Those passages also
which speak of the "lost," as for example St. Paul's
words at the commencement of his epistle to the
Romans, that "as many as have sinned without law
shall perish without law, and as many as have sinned
in the law shall be judged by the law,"[2] are not the
declaration of the final lot of any, but of the state of
all by nature, till through union with Christ they
are made partakers of His redemption. In this lost
state some are held far longer than others, and therefore are in a special sense "the lost,"[3] as compared
with the firstborn, who are made partakers of the first
resurrection. But all the saved have once been lost;[4]

---

[1] S. Luke xv. 4, 8.   [2] Rom. ii. 12.

[3] 2 Cor. iv. 3; τοὺς ἀπολλυμένους, sometimes translated "them
that perish," as in 1 Cor. i. 18, and 2 Cor. ii. 15.

[4] S. Luke xv. 24, 32.

for the Son of Man is come to seek and save that
which was lost.[1] The fact therefore that of these lost,
some are lost for a longer or a shorter period, proves
nothing against their final restoration ; for the Good
Shepherd must " go after that which is lost, until He
find it."

There are however other passages which are relied
on as unquestionably affirming never-ending punishment.   That they do teach us that those who here
reject the gospel do by their present rejection of
Christ lose a glory, which, if now lost, is lost for
ever, and do further bring upon themselves a judgment of darkness and anguish unspeakable, is, I
believe, the positive teaching of the New Testament.
Once let us, who hear the gospel, while we are in
this life sell our birthright, and then though like
Esau we may cry " with a great and exceeding bitter
cry," the glory of the first-born is for ever gone from
us, and we shall find no place or means for reversing
our choice, though when too late we seek to do so
carefully with tears.   Once lost, the birthright is for
ever lost.   But I do not on this account believe that
even the Esaus have therefore no blessing ; for I
read, " By faith Isaac blessed both Jacob and Esau
concerning things to come ;"[2] and so while the birthright is for ever lost, Esau yet has hope as " concerning things to come," and will one day get a
blessing, though never the blessing of the despised

---

[1] S. Luke xix. 10.   [2] Heb. xi. 20.

birthright. Only if we here suffer with Christ shall
we reign with Him; only if like Him we lose our
life, shall we save it for the kingdom. Still these
solemn texts, which speak of grievous loss, do not, I
believe, countenance or teach the current doctrine
of never-ending torments. I confess I cannot
perfectly explain all these texts. The exact sense
of some of them may yet be open to question.
But all who are familiar with Biblical controversies
know that this is not a difficulty which is peculiar to
the question of eternal punishment, for there is
scarcely a doctrine of our faith which at first sight
does not seem to clash more or less with some other
plain scripture; the proof of which is to be seen in
the existence of those countless sects, which have
divided and yet divide Christendom. And when I
remember how the opening of God's method of salvation has already solved for me unnumbered difficulties,—when I think how the further mystery of
the firstborn unveils yet deeper depths of God's
purpose,—I can well believe that what yet seems
contradictory will with further light be found to be
in perfect accordance with the tenour of the gospel.
And just as evil in Nature and Providence, which is
inexplicable, does not shake my faith that God is
love, or that Nature and Providence are the work of
One Supreme Intelligence, who is overruling all
apparent anomalies in accordance with an unerring
scheme of perfect love and wisdom: so the yet un-
solved difficulties of Scripture do not shake my faith

in that purpose of God which plainly is revealed to us. One part of God's Word cannot really contradict another.

Let us then look at the texts which are chiefly relied on as teaching the doctrine of everlasting punishment. It is remarkable that they are in every case the words of our Lord Himself.

(i) There is, first, the passage respecting the sin against the Holy Ghost, which our Lord declares "shall not be forgiven, neither in this world, nor in that which is to come."[1] From this it is concluded that the punishment for this sin must be never-ending. But does the text say so? The whole passage is as follows:—"Wherefore I say unto you, all manner of sin and blasphemy shall be forgiven unto men; but the blasphemy against the Spirit[2] shall not be forgiven unto men. And whosoever speaketh a word against the Son of Man, it shall be forgiven him; but whosoever speaketh against the Holy Ghost, it shall not be forgiven him, neither in this age,[3] nor in the coming one." These words, so far from proving the generally received doctrine, that sin not forgiven here can never be forgiven, distinctly assert,—first, that all manner of sin and blasphemy shall be forgiven unto men,—secondly, that some sins, those, namely, against the Son of Man, can be

---

[1] S. Matt. xii. 32; S. Mark iii. 29; S. Luke xii. 10. The words in S. Mark, which our version renders, "hath never forgiveness," in the original are, οὐκ ἔχει ἄφεσιν εἰς τὸν αἰῶνα.

[2] ἡ τοῦ πνεύματος βλασφημία.   [3] αἰών.

forgiven, apparently in this age,—and thirdly, that
other sins, against the Holy Ghost, cannot be forgiven either here or in the coming age; which last
words surely imply that some sins not here forgiven
may be forgiven in the coming age, the sin or blasphemy against the Holy Ghost not being of this
number. This is what the text asserts : and it explains
why God has so long withheld the general outpouring
of His promised Spirit; for man cannot reject or speak
against the Spirit, until the Spirit comes to act upon
him. God has two ways of teaching men ; first by
His Word, the letter or human form of truth, that is
the Son of Man, in which case a man may reject
God's call without knowing that he is really doing
so ; the other, in and by the Spirit, which convinces
the heart, which therefore cannot be opposed without
leaving men consciously guilty of rejecting God.
To reject this last cuts man off from the life and
light of the coming world. This sin therefore is not
forgiven, " neither in this age, nor in the coming
one." But the text says nothing of those " ages to
come,"[1] elsewhere revealed to us; much less does it
assert that the punishment of sin not here forgiven
is never-ending.

When therefore we remember how our Lord has
taught us to forgive, " not until seven times, but
until seventy times seven ;"[2] and when we see the
length and breadth of this commandment, that it
is bidding us forgive as God forgives, not only till

[1] Eph. ii. 7.   [2] S. Matt. xviii. 22.

seven times seven, that is the " seven times seven
years," which make the Jubilee,[1] but " unto seventy
times seven," that is a decade of Jubilees, the mystic
" seventy weeks," which " are determined to finish the
transgression, and to make an end of sins, and to
make reconciliation for iniquity, and to bring in
everlasting righteousness, and to seal up the vision
and prophecy, and to anoint the Most Holy;"[2]—words
which surely have had an inceptive fulfilment in the
first coming of our Lord, but which, like so many
other prophecies of His coming and kingdom, wait
until another coming and another age for a yet more
glorious accomplishment ;—when we remember that
this is the forgiveness which God approves, we may be
pardoned for believing that the threatening, " It shall
not be forgiven, neither in this age, nor in the coming
one," does not measure or exhaust the possibilities of
God's forgiveness. " I believe" indeed " in the Holy
Catholic Church, the resurrection of the body, and the
life everlasting ;" but I also " believe in the forgiveness of sins," even to the end, as long as God is a
Saviour and there is any sin to need forgiveness.

(ii) Again we are referred to the text, " The
wrath of God abideth on him,"[3] as another proof of
never-ending punishment. But the words do not prove
it. The context is, " He that believeth on the Son
hath everlasting life, and he that believeth not the
Son shall not see life, but the wrath of God abideth

<hr />

[1] Lev. xxv. 8.   [2] Dan. ix. 24.
[3] S. John iii. 36.

on him." The passage speaks of man's state by
nature and grace, and of the results of being possessed by faith or unbelief. Faith receives eternal
life: unbelief rejects it; and man so long as he is in
unbelief cannot see life, but has God's wrath still
resting on him. But an unbeliever, though, while
he is such, God's wrath abides upon him, may pass
by faith out of the wrath to life and blessedness. If
it were not so, all would be lost; for the lie of the
serpent has possessed us all, and we are all "by
nature children of wrath even as others." This text
therefore cannot bear the sense some put upon
it. If it could, no man once an unbeliever could
have any hope of life or deliverance. All gospel-
preaching would be in vain, if the unbeliever
could not become a believer. That this text however should be quoted on this subject is significant,
and shews the measure of light which has decided
this question.

(iii) Far more difficult is the very awful passage
which speaks of hell, "where their worm dieth not,
and the fire is not quenched."[1] But both the context
of the passage, and the Old Testament use of the
words, convince me that the ordinary interpretation
cannot be the true one. As to the context, the words
which are relied on as teaching the doctrine of never-
ending punishment are directly connected by the
conjunction "For" with a general statement as to

S. Mark ix. 42-50.

sacrifice.   The whole passage runs thus:—" And
whosoever shall offend one of these little ones that
believe in me, it is better for him that a millstone
were hanged about his neck, and he were cast into
the sea.   And if thy hand offend thee, cut it off; it
is better for thee to enter into life maimed, than
having two hands to go into hell, into the fire that
never shall be quenched;[1] where their worm dieth
not, and the fire is not quenched.   And if thy foot
offend thee, cut it off; it is better for thee to enter
halt into life, than having two feet to be cast into
hell, into the fire that never shall be quenched;
where their worm dieth not, and the fire is not
quenched.   And if thine eye offend thee, pluck it
out; it is better for thee to enter into the kingdom of
God with one eye, than having two eyes to be cast
into hell-fire; where their worm dieth not, and the
fire is not quenched.   For every one shall be salted
with fire, and every sacrifice shall be salted with salt.
Salt is good, but if the salt have lost his saltness,
wherewith will ye season it?   Have salt in yourselves, and have peace one with another."   Take
the ordinary interpretation, and there is no connection between never-ending punishment and the
law here quoted respecting salt in sacrifice.   But as
spoken by our Lord the fact or law respecting the
Meat-offering is the reason and explanation of what
is said respecting hell-fire,—" For every one must

[1] τὸ πῦρ τὸ ἄσβεστον.

be salted with fire, and every sacrifice must be salted with salt."

Here as elsewhere the law throws light on the gospel, nor can these words be understood until the exact nature of the offering which our Lord refers to is apprehended. Salt, in its nature sharp and biting, yet preserving from corruption, was expressly required in every Meat-offering;[1] this Meat-offering itself being an adjunct to the Burnt-offering, and, like it, not a Sin-offering, but a "sweet savour," and offered for acceptance;[2] the Burnt-offering shadowing the fulfilment of man's duty toward God; the Meat-offering, his duty toward his neighbour; both of which have been fulfilled for us in Christ, and are to be fulfilled by grace in us His members, as it is written, "That the righteousness of the law might be

[1] Lex. ii. 13.

[2] The offerings appointed by the Lord were (as I have already noticed,) divided into two distinct classes,—first, the sweet-savour offerings, which are all offered for acceptance; and secondly, those offerings which were not of a sweet savour, and which were required as an expiation for sin. The first class, comprising the Burnt-offering, the Meat-offering, and the Peace-offering, were offered on the brazen altar which stood in the court of the tabernacle. The second class, the Sin and Trespass-offerings, were not consumed on the altar, but were burnt on the earth without the camp. In the first class the faithful Israelite gives a sweet offering to the Lord; in the other the offering is charged with the sin of the offerer. In the Burnt-offering, the Meat-offering, and the Peace-offering, the offerer came for acceptance as a worshipper. In the Sin and Trespass-offerings, he came as a sinner to pay the penalty of sin and trespass. Unless this distinction and the general law of the offerings be understood, the force of our Lord's words as to the "salting with fire" will not be apprehended.

fulfilled in us, who walk not after the flesh but after
the spirit."[1]   The passage which we are considering
begins with this, man's duty to his neighbour, and
the peril of offending a little one.   "It were better
that a millstone were hanged about one's neck, and
that the life which offends were even destroyed,
than that we should offend or hurt one of these little
ones."   Then comes the exhortation to sacrifice
"hand," or "foot," or "eye," lest we come into the
worse judgment, which must be known by those who
will not judge themselves.   "For," says our Lord,
thus giving the reason for self-judgment, "every
man," whether he likes it or not, if he is ever to
change his present form and rise to God, "must be
salted with fire."   This may be done as a sweet-
savour to God; though even here "every sacrifice is
salted with salt,"—for even in willing sacrifice and
service there is something sharp and piercing as
salt, namely, the correction which truth brings with
it to those who will receive it.   But if this be not
accepted, the purgation must yet be wrought, not as
a sweet-savour, but as a sin-offering, where the
bodies are burnt as unclean without the camp;
"where their worm dieth not, and the fire is not
quenched;" (the "worm" alluding to the consumption
of those parts which were not burnt with fire;) "for"
in some way "every man must be salted with fire,"
even if he be not a sweet-savour "sacrifice," which

[1] Rom. viii. 4.

is " salted with salt." But all this, so far from teaching never-ending punishment only points us back to
the law of sacrifice, and to the means which must be
used to destroy sin in the flesh, and to make us ascend
in a new and more spiritual form as offerings to
Jehovah.

And the Old Testament use of the words, " The
fire shall not be quenched," is still more conclusive
against the common interpretation. The words occur
first in the law of the Burnt-offering, where we
read " The fire shall ever be burning upon the altar :
it shall never go out ;"—literally, " it shall not be
quenched,"[1]—the words being exactly the same as
those our Lord quotes here. Here, beyond all question, the words can have nothing to do with never-
ending punishment, or indeed with wrath of any
kind ; for the Burnt-offering was one of the " sweet-
savour" offerings : they speak only of the one means,
namely, the " fire of God," by which that which was
offered to and accepted by Him as " a sweet savour "
could be made to ascend upon His altar, in token of
its acceptance by Him. To keep this fire ever alive
was one of the priest's first duties, typifying the
preservation of that spiritual fire which it is Christ's
work as Priest to kindle and keep alive, for by it
alone can we " present our bodies a living sacrifice."[2]
The other places where the words occur are the follow
ing. They are twice spoken of the overthrow of the

---

[1] Lev. vi. 13 ; πῦρ οὐ σβεσθήσεται.
[2] Rom. xii. 1, and compare S. Luke xii. 49.

first Jewish temple built by Solomon:[1] then of
Edom;[2] then of Jerusalem,[3] and of the house of the
king of Judah,[4] and the forest of the south;[5] and
lastly in the passage here quoted by our Lord from
the prophet Isaiah,[6] which speaks of the punishment of the wicked at the period of the latter-day
glory. In all these cases the words express such a
destruction as was figured in the Sin-offerings, which
were cast out and burnt without the camp as unfit
for God's altar. These are the only places in the
Old Testament where the words occur, and in every
instance except the last they manifestly cannot, and
confessedly do not, involve the idea of endless suffering. Why in this one place only is a sense to be
put upon the words, which is not only untenable in
every other similar passage of the Old Testament,
but would make one part of Scripture contradict
another.

(iv) But the passage which is perhaps most often
quoted on this question is that which speaks of the
life of the righteous and the punishment of the wicked
alike as "everlasting":—" These shall go away into
everlasting punishment, but the righteous into life
eternal."[7] The word here used, and which in our
Version is translated " eternal" and " everlasting," is
in either case the same in the original.[8] Hence it is

---

[1] 2 Kings xxii. 17, and 2 Chron. xxxiv. 25.
[2] Isa. xxxiv. 10.   [3] Jer. vii. 20, and xvii. 27.
[4] Jer. xxi. 12.   [5] Ezek. xx. 47.
[6] Isa. lxvi. 24.   [7] S. Matt. xxv. 46.
[8] *αἰώνιος*.

argued, that " whatever be the meaning of the word
in the case of the lost, the same must be its meaning
in the case of the saved ; and our certainty of never-
ending bliss for penitent believers is gone, if the
word bears not the same signification in the case of
the impenitent and unbelieving."[1]

This at first sight seems to have some weight.
Yet if it can be shewn, (as we have shewn,[2]) that the
word here used is in other Scriptures applied to what
is not eternal, we may be pardoned for thinking it
cannot mean eternal here ; the rather as, if it did,
this text would contradict other plain statements of
the same Scripture. Nor, as I have said, does this
affect the true eternity of bliss of the redeemed,
which is based on participation with Christ in His
risen life, and is distinctly affirmed in other plain
Scriptures, such as, " Neither can they die any more,
but are children of God, being children of the resurrection."[3] The truth is that this word describes not
the quantity or duration, but the quality, of that
of which it is predicated. I need not here repeat
the proofs of this. But I may add that the word
which in. this passage we translate " punishment,"[4]
and which in its primary sense means simply " prun-
ing," is that always used for a corrective discipline,
which is for the improvement of him who suffers it.

---

[1] Pastoral Letter of the Archbishop of Canterbury, dated March
14, 1864, p. 7. A similar statement is to be found in the Pastoral
Letter of the Archbishop of York. p. 14.

[2] Pp. 57–68, above.

[3] S. Luke xx. 36.   [4] κόλασις.

Those who hold the common view of the endlessness of punishment are obliged to confess this;[1] and this of itself proves that their doctrine is untenable; for any punishment, be it for a longer or a shorter time, would not be corrective discipline, but quite another thing, if it left those who were so corrected unimproved and lost for ever. May we not then from this very passage prove, that, while they are doubly blessed who go away at the first resurrection into eternal life,

[1] "Of the two words, τιμωρία and κόλασις," (says the present Archbishop of Dublin, in his *Synonyms of the New Testament*, p. 30,) "in τιμωρία, according to its classical use, the vindictive character of the punishment is the predominant thought; it is the Latin 'ultio'; punishment as satisfying the inflicter's sense of outraged justice, as defending his own honour, and that of the violated law; herein its meaning agrees with its etymology, being from τιμή, and οὖρος, ὁράω, the guardianship or protectorate of honour. In κόλασις, on the other hand, is more the notion of punishment as it has reference to the correction and bettering of him that endures it; (see Philo, *Leg. ad. Cai.* § 1.) it is 'castigatio,' and has naturally for the most part a milder use than τιμωρία. Thus we find Plato (*Protag.* 323 E) joining κολάσεις and νουθετήσεις together: and the whole passage to the end of the chapter is eminently instructive as to the distinction between the words; . . . . with all which may be compared an instructive chapter in Clement of Alexandria, (*Strom.* iv. 24; and again vii. 16,) where he defines κολάσεις as μερικαὶ παιδεῖαι, and τιμωρία as κακοῦ ἀνταπόδοσις. And this is Aristotle's distinction. (*Rhet.* i. 10.) . . . It is to these and similar definitions that Aulus Gellius refers, &c. (*Noct. Att.* vi. 14.)"

Having thus clearly stated and proved what the exact meaning of κόλασις is, the Archbishop proceeds as follows:—"It would be a very serious error however to attempt to transfer this distinction in its entireness to the words as employed in the New Testament;" that is, it would be a serious error to give the word its proper sense. To such shifts are even learned and good men driven by their traditional views respecting endless punishment.

they are not wholly unblessed whom the Lord yet
cares to punish ;[1] the rather as He has shewn us, from
the first fall till now, that His changeless way is to
make even the curse a blessing.

(v) Another text often quoted on this question is,
—"Good were it for that man, if he had not been
born."[2] This it is said is a proof of never-ending
punishment, since it would be good to be born, if,
even after ages of suffering, men could at last be
restored to see God. Surely the words declare an
awful doom : an awful warning too they are to those
now near Christ. And yet as in the doom pronounced
upon our first parents, which as far as it was addressed to them had not one ray of light or word of
promise in it,—for all that God said to the woman
was sorrow, pain, humiliation ; all that He said to
the man was curse, death, ruin, desolation ; and
only in His curse upon the serpent was any promise
of the woman's seed given,[3]—this woe upon Judas,
which seems as dark as night, may yet consist with
purposes of mercy, of which in these words we find
no intimation. The fall of Judas, even as that of
our first parents, which in God's wisdom opened a
way for the fulfilment of that "purpose and grace
which was given us in Christ Jesus before the world
began,"[4] spite of its attendant judgment may not
only bring in higher good, but like Israel's fall,
which has been "the riches of the world,"[5] may

[1] Heb. xii. 6, 7.   [2] S. Matt. xxvi. 24.
[3] Gen. iii. 14-1?.   [4] 2 Tim. i. 9.   [5] Rom. xi. 12.

x 2

even end in the restoration of the fallen one to more secure blessedness. It is surely significant that one and the same awful prophecy is by the inspired writers of the New Testament applied to Judas and Israel.[1] If therefore the one is not a type or figure of the other, the two are in some way connected most intimately. And yet Israel, of whom it is said, "Let their eyes be darkened that they may not see, and bow down their back alway," (words which in the Psalm immediately precede the passage which is quoted by St. Peter in reference to the traitor Judas,) though hated for awhile, and "as concerning the gospel enemies for our sakes, are yet beloved for the fathers' sakes,"[2] and shall be restored one day, and "brought up out of their graves,"[3] "for the gifts and calling of God are without repentance."[4] And so the betrayer here, of whom the same passage is quoted, "Let his habitation be desolate, and let no man dwell therein," and whose "fall," like Israel's, has been the "riches of the world," may yet more shew the Lord's riches. It is no unreasonable inference, that, as the same prophecy applies to both, their ends shall not be wholly dissimilar. Certainly some of the threatenings upon Israel,—such as, "I will utterly forget you, and I will forsake you;"[5] nay even

[1] Compare Psalm lxix. 23, 25, with Rom. xi. 10, and Acts i. 19, 20. The same passage is applied by S. Paul to Israel, and by S. Peter to Judas.

[2] Rom. xi. 28.

[3] Ezek. xxxvii. 12.   [4] Rom. xi. 29.

[5] Jer. xxiii. 39. See the yet stronger language in Deut. xxx. 18.

such words as those of our Lord Himself, " If thou
hadst known in this thy day the things which belong
to thy peace ; but now are they hid from thine
eyes,"[1]—if less awful than the woe pronounced on
Judas, are dark enough, had no other light been
poured on them. And so these words to Judas might
forbid all hope, were there no other words of the
same Lord to make us hope for all men. It is
because there are such words, that I hesitate to put
a sense upon this woe on Judas, which shall make it
contradict other no less true and weighty words of
the same Saviour.

Let us then look again more closely at these
words. While surely applying first to Judas, like all
Christ's words they have a wider meaning. In the
passage referred to,—" The Son of Man goeth, as it
is written of Him ; but woe to that man, by whom
the Son of Man is betrayed : it had been good for
that man if he had not been born,"—two men, and
only two, are spoken of; the " Son of Man," and
" that man " by whom the Son of Man is betrayed.
Are not these in substance " the old man " and " the
new," " man " and " the Son of Man," of whom the
one is always the betrayer of the other. Of these
the one is the man of sin, the son of perdition, who
cannot be saved, but must die and go to his own
place; for flesh and blood cannot inherit the kingdom, neither doth corruption inherit incorruption.

[1] S. Luke xix. 42.

Good had it been for this man, if he had not been born; but better is it that he has been born, that God might bring in better things.[1] Good had it been, if there had been no sin and fall, but better is it that there has been a fall, " for where sin abounded, grace did much more abound."[2] The evil shall work for good, and pass away; while the results shall be for ever glorious. For all that rose in Adam falls in Christ, even as all that fell in Adam rose again in Christ. The evil is only for awhile. "I have seen the wicked in great power, and spreading himself abroad like a green bay-tree; yet he passed away, and lo, he was not: yea, I sought him, but he could not be found."[3]

(vi) There is yet another text sometimes quoted on this subject. The words to the Rich Man in hell, that "there is a great gulf fixed, so that they cannot pass who would come from thence,"[4] are said to shut out all hope for a lost soul, when it has once entered into the place of torment. But is it so? Disciples have before now misunderstood the Lord. The question is, Are those, who thus interpret these words, under-

[1] It ought not to be overlooked, too, that in the passage under consideration, "Good were it for that man if he had not been born," the word we translate "good" is καλὸν, not ἀγαθόν. This surely is not by chance. And I think I see an obvious reason for the choice of the word καλὸν here rather than ἀγαθόν. The καλὸν may be missed, while the ἀγαθὸν may by Almighty grace be yet obtainable.

[2] Rom. v. 20.

[3] Psa. xxxvii. 35, 36.

[4] S. Luke xvi. 26.

standing or only misunderstanding this most solemn
parable? What is its aim? It is a similitude of
something; for all the parables are similitudes, even
though, like the the parables of the Prodigal Son, and
the Unjust Steward, both of which are in direct connection with this one, they are uttered, as is usual
with St Luke, like simple narratives, always beginning with, "A certain man," or "There was a certain
man." Of what, then, is this parable of the Rich
Man a similitude? Whom does the Rich Man represent? Who is the poor neglected beggar full of
sores, to whom the very dogs without shew more pity
and kindness than the Rich Man? Both the connection of the parable, and its particulars throughout, shew that its awful warning is addressed, not so
much to the godless world, as to those who here en-
joy the greatest privileges. Observe the particulars
stated respecting the Rich Man. He was one of
Abraham's seed, one who even in hell could not forget his election, but still cried, "Father Abraham."
He was "clothed in purple and fine linen," the raiment of the kingdom, and, as a child of the kingdom, he "fared sumptuously every day," while Lazarus,
whose name means simply "*needing help*," was lying
at his door a mass of sores, loathsome and in want,
and yet uncared for and unpitied by him who enjoyed
so many blessings. Who are these two men? If,
with Augustine and other great teachers of the early
Church, we take the dispensational view, the Rich
Man is the Jew; the poor beggar at his gate is the

lost Gentile.[1]   In the one we see the children of the
kingdom, who as such were clothed in purple and
fine linen, and fared sumptuously every day, and yet
cared nothing for the Gentile world which lay close
at their door in spiritual want and wretchedness : in
the other we have the Gentile world, lost, full of
sores, and lacking everything.   The one, even in
hell, yet claiming to be Abraham's seed, and of
whose brethren Abraham says himself, "They have
Moses and the prophets," and "If they believe not
Moses and the prophets, neither will they be persuaded though one rose from the dead ; " the other,
brought through death, as dead sinners, into God's
rest, into those very privileges of which the good fare
and fine raiment of the Rich Man were but the type
and figure.   Such substantially is surely the lesson of
this parable, though I could never confine it, or any
other parable of our Lord's, to the old Jew and Gentile only, first, because " no prophecy of Scripture is
of private interpretation," and also because the Jew,
as Abraham's son, is himself the type of those who
by grace have now been brought into the place of
children of the kingdom, while the poor Gentile beggar is yet the pattern of those, who, though full of
sores, are yet the " poor " and the " mourners," whom
Christ calls " blessed," and who " shall be comforted."
What the parable teaches therefore is just that truth,
which the elect are so slow to believe, that the child-

[1] Augustin. *Quæst. Evang.* ii. 38, 39 ; Greg. M. *Hom.* 40, *in
Evang.*

ren of the kingdom, if unloving, shall spite of all
present privileges be cast into outer darkness, while
lost ones, now without, shall through death come in
and rest with Abraham. The Jews would not believe
it in their day. How could God be faithful if they
were cast out? The children of the kingdom now,
those who judge their state Godwards, not by their
love, that is their likeness to their Lord, but by their
privileges, by the fact that God has given them such
rich and precious blessings in Christ Jesus, are slow
to believe, that, spite of their blessings, they may be
cast out. Yet this is the solemn teaching of the
parable. It is one of Abraham's seed who is in hell;
one of the elect people, and not a poor outcast.

And yet "the great gulf fixed," which severs those
who once were nigh but are now cast out, though utterly impassable for man, is not so for " Him who
hath the key of David, who openeth and no man
shutteth, and shutteth and no man openeth, who
hath the keys of death and hell; " [1] and who, as He
has Himself broken the bars of death for men, can
yet " say to the prisoner, Go forth; to them that are
in darkness, Shew yourselves." [2] Who are we, to say
that the gulf, impassable to man, cannot be passed
by Christ, or that He cannot bring the last prisoner
safely back, even out of the lowest prison? As well
might we argue that because " the Ethiopian cannot
change his skin, or the leopard his spots," [3]—because

[1] Rev. i. 18, and iii. 7. [2] Isa. xlix. 9.
[3] Jer. xiii. 23.

the evil man can never by his own act make himself
good,—therefore God can never change him. The
firstfruits are a proof what God can do. I know
what He has done for the elect, who were " by nature
children of wrath, even as other men; "[1] and He has
said, "O death, I will be thy plagues; O hell, I will
be thy destruction; "[2] and therefore this parable,
awful as it is to me, as one who by grace am now
called to eat of the fat things of God's house and
wear the fine raiment,—because it shews how all
these blessings may be abused, and only aggravate.
my condemnation, if I am selfish and unloving,—
yet by no means proves that, awful as the judgment
is, there is no hope for those who suffer it. There
surely is hope for the Jews, though of them, and as
a warning to them, this word was first spoken. And
so surely, because God is God, there yet is hope, even
for those who shall suffer the sorest judgment.[3]

---

[1] Eph. ii. 3.   [2] Hos. xiii. 14.

[3] I subjoin what Stier, one of the most approved and spiritual
of modern commentators, and himself an advocate of the doctrine
of endless punishment, says respecting this parable. Having shewn
that this hell and torment of the Rich Man cannot refer to " the
place and condition of the eternally damned," as it only describes
the state before the resurrection, (*Words of the Lord Jesus*, vol. iv.
p. 222: there is more to the same effect, p. 233,) he says of Abraham's words, " The repelling answer hints at the justice and well-
adjusted design of love in the torments which *for the present* " (the
italics are Stier's) " are rigidly fixed." (Id. *ibid.* p. 209.) He then
sums up the general teaching of the parable as follows :—" The
enigma of the buried Rich Man, unrightly called wicked, and of
Lazarus, covered with sores and with contempt, is well worth the
attentive notice of all whom we too readily term *worthy and estim-*

Meanwhile Abraham's words have surely a solemn lesson for those " brethren of the Rich Man who have not yet come into the place of torment." " They have Moses and the prophets : let them hear them ;" and " If they believe not Moses and the prophets, neither will they be persuaded though one rose from the dead." We can apply all this to the brethren of the Jew, who would not believe or imitate God's love to Gentile sinners, even though the Friend of sinners, whom they had condemned, rose from the dead and gathered sinners to Him. But does it

able people. It is especially intended for them. The external riches are a figure of the internal, and the sores, by which the body is purified, signify something analogous in regard to the soul. . . . . Those who are warned in this parable . . . are the proud sitters in our most holy Christian sanctuary. How many a Menkenian," (this would be better understood in England if he had said, "a Darbyite,") . . . . . . "clothes himself in such priestly and royal attire, looking down upon the poor around who can go no higher than to pray for the forgiveness of sins ! . . . Such people have repented once, and therefore they are Abraham's children. But they have gradually come to neglect daily repentance and contrition, till the complete old man emerges out of their regenerate state once more, and now acts his pride in the garments of a Christian. . . . . Happy the sinner whose sins break out for his spiritual healing. Thrice happy would that proud and rich sinner be if he could become in time a poor Lazarus in God's sight, before his rich garments are torn off, and his full table disfurnished for ever. Woe to the converted sinner, if the poison still remaining should break out in the disease of spiritual pride, and he too should become a *rich man.*" (*Words of the Lord Jesus,* vol. iv. p. 248.) And he adds in a note, " In *the carnal-spiritual life* a man lives in honour and joy, and is clothed in purple like the Rich Man. Dying to this higher life of carnality he becomes poor, hungry, full of sores and tribulations, like Lazarus." (Id. *ibid.* p. 249.) This witness is true. May Abraham's sons give ear to it.

not equally apply to those who at this day, though
children of the kingdom, through their blind self-
love are in danger of the second death, and who will
not hear of any possible resurrection for any out of
it ?   Is it not written, " They have Moses and the
prophets : let them hear them " ?   What do Moses
and the prophets say of the redemption of the lost,
and of those whose inheritance does not come back at
the Sabbatic year of rest, but only at the Jubilee ?
What says the law in all its teaching as to the first-
fruits, and in its appointments for cleansing and redemption to be wrought at different seasons ?   And
what say the prophets as to the restoration of Sodom
and her daughters, and other lost ones, who when they
wrote were " aliens to the commonwealth of Israel,
strangers to the covenants of promise, without hope,
and without God," who yet in due time should be
visited ?   What is the answer when Moses now is
quoted on this point, or when some promise from
the prophets is referred to ?   " Oh, we cannot take
types or shadows for proof ; and these words quoted
from the prophets are so obscure that we can base
no certain doctrine on them."   So the brethren of the
Rich Man will not hear.   But if they hear not Moses
and the prophets, neither would they be persuaded
though one came to them even from the second death.

(vii) But all this, it is said, is opposed to the
obvious sense of Scripture ; and Scripture having been
given for simple and unlettered men, the simplest
sense must be the true one : at all events any sense

which is not obvious cannot be relied on. This objection is urged by some as though it were unanswerable. But is the so-called obvious sense of our Lord's words always the right one? Let any one consider the New Testament quotations from the Old, and say whether the passages so quoted are applied or interpreted in their obvious sense. Have we not seen also that again and again, as in our Lord's words respecting leaven, and eating His flesh, and buying a sword, and the sleep of Lazarus, and the destroying and rebuilding of the temple,—not to speak of His usual parabolic style, which was expressly used to hide even while it revealed heavenly mysteries,[1] —the so-called obvious or literal sense is beyond all question not the true one. Besides the difficulty on this point, as we have seen, is that Scripture seems to bear two different testimonies, here saying that the wicked shall be condemned and perish; there declaring that all death shall be done away. God's two ministrations of law and gospel, and the reason for each, if we understand His purpose in them, explain the difficulty. But understood or not, the fact remains, that Scripture on this point contains apparent contradiction. Those therefore who speak so glibly of "the obvious sense of Scripture" forget how many texts must be ignored, before the doctrine of never-ending punishment can be shewn to be the mind of God. What, to take one instance, is the

[1] S. Matt. xiii. 10–14.

"obvious meaning" of such words as these:—"Death
reigned from Adam to Moses, even over them that
had not sinned after the similitude of Adam's transgression, who is a figure of Him that was to come. But
not as the offence, so also is the free-gift.   For
if through the offence of one the many be dead,
much more the grace of God, and the gift by grace,
which is by one man, Jesus Christ, hath abounded
unto the many.   And not as it was by one that
sinned, so is the gift ; for the judgment was by one
to condemnation, but the free gift is of many offences
unto justification.   For if by one man's offence death
reigned by one ; much more they which receive abundance of grace, and of the gift of righteousness, shall
reign in life by one, Jesus Christ.   Therefore as by
the offence of one judgment came upon all men to
condemnation ; even so by the righteousness of one
the free gift came upon all men unto justification of
life.   For as by one man's disobedience the many
were made sinners, so by the obedience of one shall
the many be made righteous.   Moreover the law
entered that the offence might abound ; but where
sin abounded, grace did much more abound : that as
sin hath reigned unto death, even so might grace
reign, through righteousness, unto eternal life, by
Jesus Christ our Lord." [1]   What, I ask, is the "obvious meaning " of these words ?   Can a partial salvation exhaust the fulness of the blessing which St.
Paul declares so unequivocally ?   Must we not dis-

[1] Rom. v. 14–21.

tort his teaching if we try to make it say that the
redemption in Christ is less wide in its results than
the fall of Adam? Is not the argument of the passage just the reverse? Does not the Apostle, by his
repeated "much more," [1] shew again and again that
the redemption and salvation is far greater than the
ruin? The language seems chosen to obviate the
possibility of misapprehension. Why then not receive the teaching in its plain and obvious sense?
Because other words of Holy Scripture speak just as
plainly of a "wrath to come" and a "lake of fire"
for "ages of ages." And the Church's children, since
her fall, having like Israel of old despised prophesy-
ings, and lacking therefore the necessary light, which
this "key of knowledge" [2] would have given them,
have cut the knot they could not untie, by denying
one half of Scripture to uphold the other half; choos-
ing, as was natural, (for men under law can only
know God as inflicting its penalty,) that half which
spoke of condemnation. For indeed the Word alone
will never open out God's mind. We may even be
hardened by the letter in some wretched misapprehension. Only by His Spirit can we really understand God's thoughts. Thus, and thus only, can we
be "made able ministers of the New Testament; not
of the letter, but of the spirit;" able to shew how
while "the letter killeth, the spirit giveth life." [3]
For it is in Scripture as in the books of Nature and

[1] Verses 15, 17, 20.　　　　　[2] Luke xi. 52.
[3] 2 Cor. iii. 6.

Providence. Sense-readings will never solve the
difficulty. Who, as he looks for the first time at
death, would believe, that this and this only is the
way to fuller, better, life? The fact is, it is not
enough to have a revelation. We need eyes also and
hearts to read that revelation. And those, who have
most studied any of the books which God has given
us, know that so far from the obvious sense being in
every case the true one, all our sense-readings are
more or less fallacious and untrustworthy, and must
be corrected again and again, if we would possess the
real truth. Some have proved this in one field,
some in another. All must prove it if they will
go onward to perfection.

(viii) There is yet one other objection. It may
be said,—If you go so far as to hope for the final
salvation of all men, irrespective of what they have
done or have been here, why not go further, and say
that devils may be saved, for if Old Adam can be
redeemed, why not lost spirits also? Have not bad
men the devil's nature in them? Are they not called
"the children of the wicked one"?[1] Is not the
same evil nature in all God's children, till it is
slain?[2] Yet has not the Lord died for all, that by
His death He might destroy that evil nature and
deliver them? And if this nature can be slain and
changed[3] in us, why not in Satan and the fallen

---

[1] S. Matt. xiii. 38.   [2] Eph. ii. 3.

[3] Notice the language, "*perish* AND *be changed*," used in reference
to present nature, in Heb. i. 11, 12.

angels? Shall the Jews be saved, whom our Lord
calls "serpents" and "vipers,"[1] and of whom He
says, "Ye are of your father the devil,"[2] "How can
ye escape the damnation of hell;" and shall God
have no salvation for those, who, though now lost,
have once been "perfect in beauty, full of wisdom"?[3]
Was not Satan "the anointed cherub, which cover-
eth, with every precious stone upon him;" and is he
not, though "his heart was lifted up because of his
beauty, and he has corrupted himself by reason of
his brightness,"[4] yet a fallen son, against whom
"even Michael, the archangel, durst not bring a
railing accusation, but said, The Lord rebuke thee."[5]
Where do we read that there can be no hope for
such? Is it not rather distinctly written, that
though "the Lord shall punish the host of the high
ones which are on high, and they shall be gathered
in a pit and shut up in prison, yet after many days
they shall be visited"?[6] Are not therefore "the
dragons and the deeps" called to "praise the
Lord;"[7] yea, are not "the depths laid up in storehouses"?[8] And who is that king who builds the city
of confusion, who has God's prophet for his servant
and his teacher, who for his pride is as a beast till
seven times pass over him, who yet at last regains
his reason and his kingdom;[9] that king of whom the

---

[1] S. Matt. xxiii. 33.   [2] S. John, viii. 44.
[3] Ezek. xxviii. 12.   [4] Ezek. xxviii. 14–17.
[5] S. Jude 9.   [6] Isa. xxiv. 21, 22.
[7] Psa. cxlviii. 7.   [8] Psa. xxxiii. 7.   [9] Dan. iv. 34–37.

Lord says, " Nebuchadnezzar, king of Babylon, hath
devoured me, he hath crushed me, he hath made me
like an empty vessel, he hath swallowed me up like
a dragon, he hath filled his belly with my delicates,
he hath cast me out " ?[1]   The " Lord shall indeed
slay the dragon that is in the sea,"[2] and " by death
destroy him that has the power of death, that is the
devil ;"[3] but who can tell but that as death is the
way of life for us, so also it may be with that first
great offender, who " robbed his father, and said, It
is no transgression."[4]   Who but Adam and Lucifer
are the two thieves crucified with Christ?   And
though to one only was it said, " To-day shalt thou
be with me in paradise,"[5] what proof have we that
the other shall never find mercy ?   Was not the
blood of the Lamb of God shed on the cross to
" take away the sin of the world "?[6]   If so, what is
the sin of the world?   When did it commence ?
And why is not the sin of " the prince of this
world "[7] to be included in " the sin of the world "?
Is not Christ " the Head of all principality and
power,"[8] as well as " Lord both of the dead and
living."[9]   Nay more, is not even the Church called
with her Head to " judge angels "?[10]   And if the
judgment of the earth shall be its restoration,[11] why

[1] Jer. li. 34.	[2] Isa. xxvii. 1.
[3] Heb. ii. 14.	[4] Prov. xxviii 24.
[5] S. Luke xxiii. 43.	[6] S. John i. 29.
[7] S. John xiv. 30.	[8] Col. ii. 10.
[9] Rom. xiv. 9.	[10] 1 Cor. vi. 3.

[11] Psa. xcvi. 10-13, and xcviii. 3-9.

should not the judgment of angels in like manner be
their restoration, according to the promise, " By Him
to reconcile all things unto Himself, whether they be
things on earth or things in heaven "?[1]

To all this, I have nothing to say in reply ; nay,
more, I confess I cannot see that God would be dis-
honoured by such a conclusion of the great mystery.
" For if," as Paul says, " the ministration of condemnation be glory, much more shall the ministration of righteousness exceed in glory."[2]   And when
I think of the change which can be wrought in us,—
when I see that man contains all worlds, and is indeed
the hieroglyphic of the universe,—that not only the
seen and unseen, matter and spirit, time and eternity,
but hell and heaven, and the life of each, as well as
the life of earth, all are in him ; when I see that
Lucifer and Adam, the two first great offenders, the
one in his male, the other in his female, property, are
but the prototypes of the two roots of evil in us, the
one of our fallen spirit, the other of our fallen soul
and body, and that in the elect, who are first-fruits,
this hellish life can be transformed, that the selfish,
envious, proud, and wrathful spirit, which hated God,
can by a death to sin be brought back to God's image,
and that this vile body, after all its abominations
and uncleannesses, can be changed like to Christ's
glorious body, according to the power whereby He is
able to subdue even all things unto Himself ; when

[1] Col. i. 20.   [2] 2 Cor. iii. 9.

I know that He who has this power is Love, I for
one cannot limit what God shall do in grace, or say
that this or that lost one shall for ever be cut off from
His mercy.   This at least is certain, that the seven
nations of Canaan, whom Israel was called to judge,
that they might possess the land beyond Jordan, are
the appointed figure in Scripture of those " wicked
spirits in heavenly places," [1] with whom the Church's
conflict is throughout this present age.   Yet in a
later age they shared a common mercy, and one at
least of this cursed race displayed a faith not to be
found in Israel.[2] If they, so cursed, and to be
judged without pity, could yet find mercy in a later
age, shall not our enemies also, with whom we fight
with the sword of the Spirit, in due time through
judgment find mercy ?[3]   And though the Church of
this age, which, brought up like Jonah out of the
belly of hell, may like Jonah be angry, because the
judgment threatened has not fallen as it expected,
God will justify His mercy to that vast assembly,
where there are, as He says, so many who cannot
discern between their right hand and their left, not
to speak of those who are as beasts before Him.[4]

§ IV. *Concluding Remarks.*

Such then I believe is the testimony of Scripture
as to the purpose and way of God our Saviour.   That

[1] Eph. vi. 12.   [2] S. Matt. xv. 22-28.
[3] See *Appendix*, Note C, p. 190.   [4] Jonah iv. 11.

it will be judged as false doctrine by those, who, like Israel of old, can see no purpose of God beyond their own dispensation, is as certain as that Israel slew the prophets, and rejected the counsel of God toward sinners of the Gentiles; that it will be hateful also to fallen spirits may be seen from the way in which proud souls in every age rebel against the gospel. Their thought is that they shall continue for ever. Very humbling is it to think that all their pride and rebellion must be overthrown. Even with true souls, who have been teaching another doctrine, there must be special difficulties in receiving a truth which proves them to have been in error. Now therefore, as of old, Samaritans know Christ as "Saviour of the world,"[1] while masters of Israel reject Him in this character. For teachers to learn is to unlearn; and this is not easy. Nor can we expect that those, who occupy the chief seats in the synagogue, will readily descend from them and humble themselves, not only to take the place of learners, but to be reproached for doing so. How can masters of Israel eat their own words? Even those who are willing to be taught are fearful. The consciousness that they are liable to err, and may be deceived, makes them cling to that which they are accustomed to. All these things, and still more our natural hard thoughts of God, are against the spread of the doctrine set forth in these pages. But if it be God's purpose, it

---

[1] S. John iv. 42.

shall stand, and each succeeding age shall make it more manifest. God will at last surely cure all men of their mistrust of Him.

Meanwhile He says, "He that hath my word, let him speak my word faithfully. What is the chaff to the wheat? saith the Lord."[1] I do not fear therefore that the declaration of God's righteousness and love will lead men, as some suppose, to think less of Him. "We are saved by hope;"[2] not by fear. It is the lie, that He is a destroyer and does not love us, which has kept and yet keeps souls from Him. And though some argue that the doctrine of final restitution, even supposing it to be true, ought not to be whispered, except with great reserve, because men will abuse it, I cannot but think their prudence unwise, and that the truth, when God has revealed it, may be trusted to do its own work. Of course this truth, like every other, may be abused. What good thing is there which may not be perverted? The Bible and the gospel itself may be wrested to men's destruction, and Christ Himself be made a savour of death to those He died for. But surely this is no reason for locking up the Bible or the gospel, or for keeping back or denying any truth which God has graciously revealed to us. And when I think of past objections to the gospel, that if grace is preached, men will abuse it and sin that grace may more abound,—when I remember how the doctrine of

[1] Jer. xxiii. 28.   [2] Rom. viii. 24.

justification by faith has been opposed, on the ground that it must undermine all practical godliness,—when I see how God's election, clearly as it is revealed in Holy Scripture, is denied by some, who, wiser than God, think that such a doctrine must be perilous to man and opposed to God's love and truth, —I have less faith in the supposed consequences of any doctrine, assured, that, if only it be true, its truth must in the end justify it. I rather believe that if the exactness of final retribution were understood, if men saw that so long as they continue in sin they must be under judgment, and that only by death to sin are they delivered, they could not pervert the gospel as they now do, nor abuse that preaching of the Cross which is indeed salvation.

I cannot but think too that this doctrine of final restitution would meet much of the hopeless scepticism which is abroad, and which is certainly increased by this dogma of never-ending punishment. Men turn from the gospel and from the Scriptures, not knowing what they contain, offended at the announcement, which shocks them, that God who is love consigns all but a " little flock," the " few who find the narrow way," to endless misery. Even true believers groan under the burden which this doctrine, as it is commonly received, must lay on all thoughtful and unselfish minds. " For my part," says Henry Rogers, " I fancy I should not grieve, if the whole race of mankind died in its fourth year. As far as we can see, I do not know that it would be a thing much to be

lamented."[1] "The same gospel," says Isaac Taylor,
"which penetrates our souls with warm emotions,
dispersive of selfishness, brings in upon the heart a
sympathy that tempts us often to wish that itself
were not true, or that it had not taught us so to
feel."[2] Even more affecting are the words of Albert
Barnes, as a witness to the darkness of the ordinary
orthodox theology:—" These and a hundred difficulties meet the mind, when we think on this great
subject; and they meet us when we endeavour to
urge our fellow sinners to be reconciled to God, and
to put confidence in Him. I confess for one that
I feel these, and feel them more sensibly and power-
fully the more I look at them, and the longer I live.
I do not know that I have a ray of light on this
subject, which I had not when the subject first
flashed across my soul. I have read to some extent
what wise and good men have written. I have looked
at their theories and explanations. I have endea-
voured to weigh their arguments, for my whole soul
pants for light and relief on these questions. But I
get neither; and in the distress and anguish of my
own spirit, I confess that I see no light whatever. I
see not one ray to disclose to me the reason why sin
came into the world, why the earth is strewed with
the dying and the dead, and why man must suffer to
all eternity."[3]

[1] Professor Henry Rogers, in *Greyson's Letters.* Letter vii. to
C. Mason, Esq., vol. i. p. 34.

[2] Isaac Taylor's *Restoration of Belief*, p. 367.

[3] Albert Barnes' *Practical Sermons*, p. 123.

Such confessions are surely sad enough ; but they do not and cannot express one thousandth part of the horror which the idea of never-ending misery should produce in every loving heart. As Archer Butler says, " Were it possible for man's imagination to conceive the horrors of such a doom as this, all reasoning about it would be at an end; it would scorch and wither all the powers of human thought."[1] Indeed human life would be at a stand, could this doctrine of endless torment be realized. Can such a doctrine then be true ? If it be, let men declare it always and in every place. But if it be simply the result of a misconception of God's Word, it is high time that the Church awake to truer readings of it.

It is not for me to judge God's saints who have gone before. Their judgment is with the Lord, and their work with their God. But when I think of the words, not of the carnal and profane, but even of some of God's dear children in that long night, when " the beast" which looked " like a lamb, but spake as a dragon," had dominion,[2]—when I find Augustine saying, that " though infants departing from the body without baptism will be in the mildest, damnation of all, yet he greatly deceives and is deceived who preaches that they will not be in damnation," meaning thereby unending punishment ;[3] or Thomas

[1] Sermons, *Second Series*, p. 383.

[2] Rev. xiii. 11.

[3] "Potest proinde rectè dici, parvulos sine baptismo de corpore eruentes in damnatione omnium mitissimâ futuros. Multum autem

Aquinas, that "the bliss of the saved may please
them more, and they may render more abundant
thanks to God for it, that they are permitted to gaze
on the punishment of the wicked;"[1] or Peter
Lombard, that "the elect, while they see the unspeakable sufferings of the ungodly, shall not be
affected with grief, but rather satiated with joy at the
sight, and give thanks to God for their own salvation;"[2] or Luther, that "it is the highest degree of
faith to believe that God is merciful, who saves so
few and damns so many; to believe Him just, who of
His own will makes us necessarily damnable;"[3]—
when I remember that such men have said such things,
and that words like these have been approved by
Christians, I can only fall down and pray that such
a night may not return, and that where it yet weighs
on men's hearts the Lord may scatter it.

fallit et fallitur, qui eos in damnatione prædicat non futuros," &c.—
De peccatorum meritis, lib. i. cap. 16, § 21. Augustine constantly
repeats this doctrine.

[1] "Unumquodque ex comparatione contrarii magis cognoscitur,
quia contraria juxta se posita magis elucescent; et ideo ut beatitudo
sanctorum eis magis complaceat, et de eâ uberiores gratias Deo
agant, datur eis ut pœnam impiorum perfectè videant."—*Summa*,
Part iii. Suppl. Quæst. 94, Art. i.

[2] "Egredientur ergo electi ad videndum impiorum cruciatus, quos
videntes non dolore afficientur, sed lætitiâ satiabuntur, agentes
gratias de suâ liberatione, visâ impiorum ineffabili calamitate."—
Sentent. lib. iv. distinct. 5, G.

[3] "Hic est fidei summus gradus, credere illum clementem, qui
tam paucos salvat, tam multos damnat, credere justum, qui suâ
voluntate nos necessario damnabiles facit," &c.—*De servo arbitrio*,
§ 23, Opp. tom. iii. fol. 176. Jhenæ, 1557.

For it is not unbelievers only that are hurt by such teaching. Those who believe it are even more injured. For our views of God re-act upon ourselves. By an eternal law, we must more or less be changed into the likeness of the God we worship. If we think Him hard, we become hard. If we think Him careless of men's bodies and souls, we shall be careless also. If we think Him love, we shall reflect something of His loving-kindness. God therefore gave us His image in His Only-Begotten Son, that " we with open face beholding as in a glass the glory of the Lord, might be changed into the same image." [1] What that image was the Gospels tell. In word and deed they shew that " God is love ; " " bearing all things, believing all things, hoping all things, enduring all things ; never failing," [2] when all around Him failed : to the end, as at the beginning, the life and hope of lost sinners. Oh blessed gospel—" He who was rich yet became poor, that we by His poverty might be rich." [3] He " who was in the form of God, and thought it not robbery to be equal with God, yet made Himself of no reputation, and took on Him the form of a servant, and was made in the likeness of men." [4] He came from life to death, from heaven to earth : " because we were in the flesh, He came in the flesh," [5] to bear our burden for us ; to take our shame and curse and death, that He might break

[1] 2 Cor. iii. 18.   [2] 1 S. John iv. 8, 16 ; 1 Cor. xiii. 7.
[3] 2 Cor. viii. 9.   [4] Phil. ii. 6, 7.
[5] Heb. ii. 14 ; 1 S. John iv. 3.

our bonds, and bring us back, in, and with, and for, Himself, to God's right hand for ever. How He did it, with what pity, truth, patience, tenderness, and love, no eye but God's yet sees fully. Our unlikeness to Him proves how little we have seen Him; for " we shall be like Him when we see Him as He is."[1] Yet what some have seen has made them new creatures. Men who lived for self have " laid down their lives,"[2] yea have " wished themselves accursed for their brethren,"[3] because His spirit possessed them, and therefore they could not but spend and be spent, like Him they loved, to save lost ones. Will the coming glory change all this? Will Christ there be another Christ from what He was here? Can He there look on ruined souls without the will to save; or is it that in glory, though the will is there, the power to save is taken from Him? And will the glory change His members too,—change them back to love their neighbour as themselves no longer? Shall a glimpse of Christ now make us long to live and die for others; and when, by seeing Him as He is, we are made like Him, shall our willingness to die and suffer for the lost be taken from us? Will this be being made like Him? If what is so generally taught is the truth,—and I can scarcely write it,—Christ there will be unlike Christ here: He will, if not unwilling, be yet unable, to save to the uttermost. Nay more,—so we are taught,—

---

[1] 1 S. John iii. 2.   [2] 1 S. John iii. 16.   [3] Rom. ix. 3.

instead of weeping over the lost, as He wept here,
He will feel no pang, while myriads of His creatures,
if not His children, are in endless torment. Then at
least He will not be " Jesus Christ, the same yesterday, to-day, and for ever." [1] Is this blasphemy?
Then who teaches it? Surely men cannot know
what they are doing when they teach such doctrine.
Do they not see how, because it is a lie, it hardens,
and must harden, even converted souls who really
believe it? For if with Christ in heaven it will be
right to look on the torments of the lost unmoved,
and to rest in our own joy, and thank God that we
are not as other men, the same conduct and spirit
cannot be evil now. Many shew they think so. The
world is lost, and they are saved; but they can live
now, as they hope one day to live with Christ, so
rejoicing in their own salvation, that they have no
pity for the crowds, who, if not yet in hell, are going
thither all around them. Even true believers are
injured more than they are aware, just in proportion as they really believe in never-ending torments.
If not almost hopeless about the removal of any very
subtle or persistent form of error, they shew that
they have little faith in the power of unwearying love
to overcome it. Why should they not allow some evil
to remain if the Lord of all permits it for ever in His
universe; or how should they expect to overcome
evil with good, when, according to their creed, God

[1] Heb. xiii. 8.

Himself either cannot or will not do so through ages
of ages? Why should they not therefore after a few
brief efforts leave the wilful and erring to their fate,
since the God of patience Himself, according to
their gospel, will leave souls unchanged, unsaved,
and unforgiven for ever? With their views they
can only judge the evil: they do not believe that it can
be overcome by good, or that those now captive to it
can and must be delivered by unfailing love and truth
and patience. Even the very preaching of the gospel
is affected by this view; for men are hurried by it
into crude and hasty work with souls,—unlike Him
who "stands at the door and knocks," [1]—by which
they often prematurely excite and thus permanently
injure the proper growth of that "new man," whom
they desire to bring forth. Blessed be God, His grace
is over all; and He is better than His most loving
children think Him; and our mistakes about Him,
though they hurt His people and the world, can
never change His blessed purpose. And His Word,
—and men would see this if they searched it more,—
in the "law of the first-fruits," in the "purpose of the
ages," and in salvation through "the cross," that is
through dissolution; above all in the face of Jesus
Christ, tells out the truth which solves the great
riddle, and shews why man must suffer while he is in
sin, that through such suffering and death he may
be brought back in Christ to God, and be re-made in
His likeness.

[1] Rev. iii. 20.

I conclude as I began. The question is, What saith the Scripture? If these hard views of God, which so many accept, are indeed the truth, let men not only believe them, but proclaim them ceaselessly. If they are, as I believe, only misconceptions of the truth, idols of man's mind, as false and contrary to the revelation God has made of Himself in Christ as the idols of stone and wood and gold and silver were to the law of Moses, may the Spirit of our God utterly destroy them everywhere, and change our darkness into perfect day. No question can be of greater moment, nor can any theology which blinks the question meet the cravings which are abroad, and which I cannot but believe are the work of God's Spirit. The question is in fact, whether God is for us or against us; and whether, being for us, He is stronger than our enemies. To this question I have given what I believe is God's answer. And my conviction is that the special opening of this truth, as it is now being opened by God Himself, everywhere, is an evident sign and witness of the passing away of present things, and of the very near and imminent judgment of apostate Christendom. A time of trial and conflict plainly is coming, between a godless spiritualism on the one hand, and on the other a so-called faith, which has lost all real experience of spirit-teaching and spirit-manifestations, whose professors therefore have nothing to fall back on but a letter or tradition, which, however true, will in carnal hands be a poor defence against a host of

lying spirits. Alas for those who in such a trial,
while calling themselves the Lord's, know nothing
of hearing His inward voice or of being taught by
His Spirit. But He yet says, " He that hath an ear,
let him hear what the Spirit saith." His grace, if
sought, is still sufficient for us. May He more
fully guide us into His own truth, and as a means
open to us yet more His Holy Scriptures, which,
like the world around, contain unknown and undiscovered treasures, even the unsearchable riches of
Christ, which are laid up for lost creatures.

I remain,

Yours most truly,

ANDREW JUKES.

POSTSCRIPT.

P.S.—I add one or two extracts from William Law, which bear more or less directly on the subject of the preceding pages. Speaking of the fall, he says,—

" I have thus shewn the glory of man's original state in Paradise, and the lamentable change that the fall has brought upon him. From a divine and heavenly creature he is so wretchedly changed as to have inwardly the nature and dark fire of the devils, and outwardly the nature of all the beasts, a slave of this outward world, living at all uncertainties amongst pains, fears, sorrows, and diseases, till his body is forced to be removed from our sight and hid in the earth.

And the reason why even the most profligate persons do not fully know and perceive their souls to be in this miserable state, is because the soul, though thus fallen, was still united to the blood of a human body, and therefore the sweet and cheering light of the sun could reach the soul, and do that for it in some degree, and for some time, which it does to the darkness, sharpness, sourness, bitterness, and wrath, which is in outward nature; that is, it could enlighten, sweeten, and clear it in a certain degree. But as this is not its own life, that is, does not arise in the soul itself, but only reaches it by means of the body, so if the soul hath in this present time got no light of its

M

own, when the death of the body breaks off its communion with the light of this world, the soul is left a mere dark, raging fire, in the state of devils.   If therefore the light of this world were to be at once extinguished, all human souls that are not in some real degree of regeneration would immediately find themselves to be nothing but the rage of fire and the horror of darkness.

Now though the light and comfort of this outward world keeps even the worst of men from any constant, strong sensibility of that wrathful, fiery, dark, and self-tormenting nature, which is the very essence of every fallen, unregenerate soul, yet every man in the world has more or less frequent and strong intimations given him that so it is with him in the inmost ground of his soul.   How many inventions are some people forced to have recourse to, to keep off a certain inward uneasiness which they are afraid of, and know not whence it comes.   Alas, it is because there is a fallen spirit, a dark aching fire within them, which has never had its proper relief, and is trying to discover itself and calling out for help at every cessation of worldly joy.

Why are some people, when under heavy disappointments or some great worldly shame, at the very brink of distraction, unable to bear themselves, and desirous of death of any kind?   It is because worldly light and comforts no longer acting sweetly upon the blood, the soul is left to its own dark, fiery, raging nature, and would destroy the body at any rate,

rather than continue under such a sensibility of its
own wrathful, self-tormenting fire.

Who has not at one time or other felt a sourness,
wrath, selfishness, envy, and pride, which he could
not tell what to do with or how to bear, rising up
without his consent, casting a blackness over all his
thoughts, and then as suddenly going off again, either
by the cheerfulness of sun and air, or some agreeable
accident, and again at times as suddenly returning
upon him?   Sufficient indications are these to every
man that there is a dark guest within him, concealed
under the cover of flesh and blood, often lulled asleep
by worldly light and amusements, yet such as will
in spite of everything shew itself, and which, if it
have not its proper cure in this life, must be his torment in eternity.   And it was because of this hidden
hell within us that our blessed Lord said when on
earth, and says now to every soul, 'Come unto me, all
ye that labour and are heavy laden, and I will give
you rest.'   For as the soul is become this self-tormenting fire only because the birth of the Son of God
was extinguished in it by our first parents, so there
is no other possible remedy for it, either in heaven
or earth, but by its coming to this Son of God to be
born again of Him.

Oh, poor unbelievers, that content yourselves with
this foundation of hell in your nature, or either seek
for no salvation, or, what is worse, turn your backs
with disregard on the One Only Saviour that God
Himself can help you to, think not of saving your-

selves: it is no more in your power than to save the
fallen spirits that are in hell. And talk not of the
mercy and goodness of God. His mercy is indeed
infinite, and His goodness above all conception; but
then the infiniteness of it consists in this that He
offered this Saviour to mankind, because in the nature
of things nothing less than this Saviour could redeem
them. Therefore to choose to rely upon some other
goodness of God beside that which He has offered
to us in Jesus Christ, is the most dreadful mistake
that can befall any man, and must, if persevered in,
leave him out of the possibility of any kind or degree
of salvation. For as the Son of God is the brightness and glory of the Father, so no soul made in the
likeness of God is capable of any degree of brightness and glory but so far as the birth of the Son of
God is in it: therefore to reject this birth, to refuse
this method of redemption, is to reject all the goodness that the Divine Nature itself hath for us." [1]

" And yet the Love that brought forth the existence of all things changes not through the fall of its
creatures, but is continually at work to bring back all
fallen nature and creature. All that passes for a time
between God and His fallen creature is but one and
the same thing, working for one and the same end,
and though this is called 'wrath,' and that called
'punishment,' 'curse,' and 'death,' it is all from the
beginning to the end nothing but the work of the
first creating Love, and means nothing else, and does

[1] *Grounds of Christian Regeneration*, pp 11-15.

nothing else, but those works of purifying fire, which must and alone can burn away all that dark evil which separates the creature from its first-created union with God. God's providence, from the fall to the restitution of all things, is doing the same thing as when He said to the dark chaos of fallen nature, 'Let there be light.' He still says, and will continue saying, the same thing, till there is no evil of darkness left in nature and creature. God creating, God illuminating, God sanctifying, God threatening and punishing, God forgiving and redeeming, are all but one and the same essential, immutable, never-ceasing working of the Divine Nature. That in God, which illuminates and glorifies saints and angels in heaven, is that very same working of the Divine Nature, which wounds, pains, punishes, and purifies, sinners upon earth. And every number of destroyed sinners, whether thrown by Noah's flood or Sodom's brimstone into the terrible furnace of a life insensible of anything but new forms of misery until the judgment day, must through the all-working, all-redeeming love of God, which never ceases, come at last to know that they had lost and have found again such a God of love as this.

And if long and long ages of fiery pain and tormenting darkness fall to the share of many or most of God's apostate creatures, they will last no longer than till the great fire of God has melted all arrogance into humility, and all that is self has died in the bloody sweat and all-saving cross of Christ, which will never give up its redeeming power till sin and sinners have no more a name among the creatures of God. And if long ages hereafter can only do that, for a soul departing this life under a load of sins, which days and nights might have done for a most hardened Pharaoh or a most wicked Nero whilst in the body, it is because, when flesh and blood are taken from it, the soul has only the strong apostate nature of fallen angels, which must have its place in that blackness of darkness of a fiery wrath that burns in them and in their kingdom.

To prevent this and make us children of the resurrection, Jesus Christ, the Only-Begotten Son of God, came into the world, and died, and rose again for us. . . . Does not this speak plainly enough what it was that man lost by his fall, namely, the birth of the Son of God in his soul? And therefore it was that the Son of God alone, and He only by the cross, could be man's Redeemer." [1]

"For in very deed the new birth is a new man, whether Christ for us, or Christ in us, which is formed by the Divine Word. And this new man is 'he that is born of God and cannot sin,' because he has no sin in his nature. This is 'he that overcometh the world,' because he is of a divine nature, and is both contrary to the world, and above it. This is he who can alone 'love his brother as himself,' because the love of God abideth in him. The old natural man is of this world, and enlightened only

[1] *Address to the Clergy,* pp. 171–173, slightly abridged.

with the light of this world : he is shut up in his
own envy, pride, and wrath, and can only escape from
these by the cross of Christ, that is by dying with
Him. This is the ' self' that our Saviour calls on
us to deny—this is the ' self' that we are to ' hate '
and ' lose,' that the kingdom of God may come in
us, that is, that God's will may be done in us. All
other sacrifices that we make, whether of worldly
goods, honours, or pleasures, are but small matters
compared to that death of self, spiritual as well as
natural, which must be made before our regeneration hath its perfect work." [1]

" Let no one therefore take offence at the opening
of this mystery, as if it brought anything new into
religion ; for it has nothing new in it ; it alters no
point of gospel-doctrine, but only sets each article of
the old Christian faith upon its true ground, pressing
nothing more than this, namely the necessity, if we
would be saved, of the opening of the life of God
within us, and of a death to that life of self which
keeps us far from God. Suffer me therefore once
more to beseech you, as I have so often said, not to
receive this mystery as a mere notion, nor, as the
world has for the most part done with the Bible, to
make it a matter of opinion or speculation. This
and every other doctrine is useless, and worse than
useless, unless it teaches that Truth can have no real
entrance into you except so far as you die to self and
to your earthly nature. The gospel says all this to

[1] *Grounds of Christian Regeneration*, pp. 69 and 99.

you in the plainest words, and the mystery only
shews you that the whole system of the universe says
the same thing.   To be a true student or disciple of
the mystery is to be a disciple of Christ; for it
calls you to nothing but the gospel, and wherever
it enters, either into the height or depth of nature,
it is only to confirm those words of Christ, ' He that
followeth me not, walketh in darkness,' and ' Unless
a man deny himself, and forsake all that he hath,
he cannot be my disciple.'   This is the philosophy
opened in this mystery.   It is not to lead you after
itself, but to compel you by every truth of nature to
turn to Christ, as the one Way, the one Truth, the
one Life and Salvation of the soul ; not as notionally
apprehended or historically known, but as experi-
mentally found, living, speaking, and working, in
your soul.   Read as long or as much as you will
of this mystery, it is all labour lost, if you intend
anything else by it, or would be anything else from
it, but a man dead to sin and to the world, that
you may live unto God through Jesus Christ our
Lord." [1]

[1] *Way to Divine Knowledge*, pp. 255-258, abridged.

APPENDIX.

NOTE A.

Scripture use of the words " death " and " destruction."

THE opinion of the annihilation of the wicked, which has at different times been held by some, as a refuge from the doctrine of never-ending punishment, is not only opposed to the whole analogy of our regeneration, which shews how death and judgment are the only way of life and deliverance for a fallen creature, but also so directly contradicts what is said of "death" in Scripture, that it is difficult to conceive how it could ever have been accepted by believers. Even before the reason of the Cross is seen, the very letter of Scripture, one might have thought, would have kept men from concluding that the " death," " destruction," and " perishing," of the wicked means their non-existence or annihilation. For what is " death "? What is " destruction "? How are these words invariably used in Holy Scripture?

First, as to "death," are any of the varied deaths, which Scripture speaks of as incident to man, his non-existence or annihilation? Take as examples the deaths referred to by St. Paul, in the sixth, seventh, and eighth chapters of the Epistle to the Romans. We read, (chapt. vi. 7,) " He that is dead is freed from sin." Is this "death," which is freedom from sin, non-existence or annihilation? Again, where the Apostle says, (chapt. vii. 9,) " I was alive without the law once, but when the commandment came, sin revived, and I died,"—was this " death," wrought in him by the law, annihilation?

Again, where he says, (chapt. viii. 6,) "To be carnally minded is death," is this death non-existence or annihilation? And again, when he says, (chapt. viii. 38,) "Neither death nor life shall separate us," is the "death" here referred to annihilation? When Adam died on the day he sinned, (Gen. ii. 17,) was this annihilation? When his body died, and turned to dust, (Gen. v. 5,) was this annihilation? Is our "death in trespasses and sins," (Eph. ii. 1, 2,) annihilation? Is our "death to sin," (Rom. vi. 11,) annihilation? When the "corn of wheat falls into the ground and dies," (S. John xii. 24,) is it annihilated; or is St. Paul right in saying, (1 Cor. xv. 37,) "That which thou sowest is not quickened except it die?" Do not these and similar uses of the word prove beyond all question, that whatever else these deaths may be, not one of them is non-existence or annihilation? Is it then the "second death" only that is annihilation? On what grounds, I ask, are we to assign a sense to this particular death which confessedly the word "death" has not and cannot have elsewhere? Where is the proof that there is and can be no resurrection from the second death?

The truth is, death for man is simply an end to, and separation from, some given form of life which he has lived in. Death to God is separation from His world of light, by the destruction, through the lie of the serpent, of the divine life of light and love in us. Death to sin, the exact converse of this, is the separation from the world of darkness, by the destruction, through the truth, of the dark life of unbelief and self-love. The death wrought by the law is the end of, and separation from, our fallen carnal life of self-sufficiency; while what is commonly called death, namely the death of the body, is simply our separation from the outward world, in which we live, as partakers of its outward life, while we are in the body. Once let us see that there are three worlds, each having its own life,—a light world, a dark world, and this outward seen world,—and then what is said in Scripture of the new birth, or of the varied deaths we pass through, becomes at once self-evident. For the only way into any world is by a birth into it, even as the only way out of any world is by a death to it. We have by sin died to God's light-world, to fall into and live in a spirit-world of darkness. We must by the truth, that is by Christ, die to this dark spirit-world, to return to live in God's light-world. The outward birth and death of the body, and its life, have only to do with the outward seen world.

For this reason it is that the word "destruction," as used in Scripture, never means annihilation. Take for instance the words of the xcth Psalm, "Thou turnest man to destruction: again Thou sayest, Come again, ye children of men." Can "destruction" here be annihilation? Is it not rather that dissolution which must take place if fallen creatures are ever to be brought back perfectly to God's kingdom. So, again, Job says, (chapt. xix. 10,) "He hath destroyed me on every side, and I am gone"; and again, (chapt. ix. 22,) "This one thing I said, He destroyeth the perfect and the wicked." But does he mean to say that he is brought to non-existence, or that the "perfect" will be so destroyed that they will exist no longer? So, again, St. Peter says, (2 Ep. iii. 6,) "The world that then was perished." So, again, of the present heavens and earth it is said, (Heb. i. 11, 12,) "They shall perish, . . . and be changed." So, again, both of Israel and Jerusalem it is said, (Deut. xxx. 18; Jer. xii. 17; xv. 6;) that they shall be "destroyed" and "perish." But does any one suppose that therefore they will be annihilated? So, again, as to the ex- pression, "them that perish," sometimes translated "the lost"; (see 2 Cor. iv. 3; 1 Cor. i. 18; 2 Cor. ii. 15;) do we not know that these "lost," though they "perish," still exist, and exist both as "lost" ones and as "saved" ones, as text on text will testify abundantly. So as to the righteous, in the well-known passage of Isaiah; (chapt. lvii. 1;) "The righteous perisheth, and no man layeth it to heart";—is this "perishing" non- existence? So, again, where we read, in Psalm lxxxiii. 16—18, "Fill their faces with shame, that they may seek thy name, O Lord: let them be confounded and troubled for ever; yea, let them be put to shame and perish; that *men*" (literally "*they*," for the word "*men*" is not in the Original,) "may know that Thou, whose name is Jehovah, art the Most High over all

you in the plainest words, and the mystery only
shews you that the whole system of the universe says
the same thing.   To be a true student or disciple of
the mystery is to be a disciple of Christ; for it
calls you to nothing but the gospel, and wherever
it enters, either into the height or depth of nature,
it is only to confirm those words of Christ, 'He that
followeth me not, walketh in darkness,' and 'Unless
a man deny himself, and forsake all that he hath,
he cannot be my disciple.'   This is the philosophy
opened in this mystery.   It is not to lead you after
itself, but to compel you by every truth of nature to
turn to Christ, as the one Way, the one Truth, the
one Life and Salvation of the soul ; not as notionally
apprehended or historically known, but as experi-
mentally found, living, speaking, and working, in
your soul.   Read as long or as much as you will
of this mystery, it is all labour lost, if you intend
anything else by it, or would be anything else from
it, but a man dead to sin and to the world, that
you may live unto God through Jesus Christ our
Lord." [1]

[1] *Way to Divine Knowledge*, pp. 255-258, abridged.

APPENDIX.

———◆◆◆———

Note A.

Scripture use of the words " death " and " destruction."

THE opinion of the annihilation of the wicked, which has at different times been held by some, as a refuge from the doctrine of never-ending punishment, is not only opposed to the whole analogy of our regeneration, which shews how death and judgment are the only way of life and deliverence for a fallen creature, but also so directly contradicts what is said of "death" in Scripture, that it is difficult to conceive how it could ever have been accepted by believers. Even before the reason of the Cross is seen, the very letter of Scripture, one might have thought, would have kept men from concluding that the " death," " destruction," and " perishing," of the wicked means their non-existence or annihilation. For what is " death "? What is " destruction "? How are these words invariably used in Holy Scripture?

First, as to "death," are any of the varied deaths, which Scripture speaks of as incident to man, his non-existence or annihilation? Take as examples the deaths referred to by St. Paul, in the sixth, seventh, and eighth chapters of the Epistle to the Romans. We read, (chapt. vi. 7,) "He that is dead is freed from sin." Is this " death," which is freedom from sin, non-existence or annihilation? Again, where the Apostle says, (chapt. vii. 9,) " I was alive without the law once, but when the commandment came, sin revived, and I died,"—was this " death," wrought in him by the law, annihilation?

" in the days of His flesh, when He had offered up prayers unto Him that was able to save Him from death," σώζειν αὐτὸν ἐκ θανάτου, (literally "*out of* death,") "He was heard in that He feared." But He was not preserved from death, but delivered out of it. Our salvation also, like our Lord's, for we are His members, is not *from* death, but *by* it, and *out of* it.

Note B.

Extracts from the Fathers.

The following extracts from some of the greatest of the Greek Fathers will sufficiently shew what were their views on this subject.

I give an extract from Origen first, as, though not the earliest, he is the best known advocate of the doctrine of Universal Restitution. He writes as follows: (*Comment. in Epist. ad Rom.* lib. viii. cap. xi.)—"Qui vero verbi Dei et doctrinæ evangelicæ purificationem spreverit, tristibus et pœnalibus purificationibus semetipsum reservat, ut ignis gehennæ in cruciatibus purget quem nec apostolica doctrina nec evangelicus sermo purgaverit, secundum illud quod scriptum est, *Et purificabo te igne ad purificationem.* Verum hæc ipsa purgatio, quæ per pœnam ignis adhibetur, quantis temporibus, quantisve sæculis, de peccatoribus exigat cruciatus, solus scire potest Ille cui Pater omne judicium tradidit. . . . Veruntamen meminisse semper debemus quod præsentem locum Apostolus quasi mysterium habere voluit, quo scilicet hujusmodi sensus fideles quique et perfecti intra semetipsos velut mysterium Dei silentio tegant, nec passim imperfectis et minus capacibus proferant."

That is,—" But he that despises the purification of the word of God, and the doctrine of the gospel, only keeps himself for dreadful and penal purifications afterwards; that so the fire of hell may purge him in torments whom neither apostolical doctrine nor gospel preaching has cleansed, according to that which is written of being 'purified by fire.' But how long this purification which is wrought out by penal fire shall endure, or for how many periods or ages it shall torment sinners, He only knows to whom all judgment is committed by the Father. . . . But we must still remember that the Apostle would have this text accounted as a secret, so that the faithful and perfect may keep their perceptions of it as one of God's secrets in silence among themselves, and not divulge it everywhere to the imperfect and those less capable of receiving it."

We find the same doctrine still more fully stated by Origen, in his work *De Principiis*, lib. i. c. 6, § 1, 2, where he quotes Psalm cx. 1, 1 Cor. xv. 25, S. John xvii. 20-23, Phil. ii. 10, and other passages of Scripture, in support of it. At the same time he did not deny, *Contr. Celsum*, lib. vi. c. 26, that the doctrine might be dangerous to the unconverted. He therefore, on the principle of reserving some things from those who might abuse them, speaks in *Hom.* xviii. *in Jerem.* § 1, of "the impossibility of being renewed except in this world." Yet in the very next homily, *Hom.* xix. *in Jer.* § 4, he calls the fear of everlasting punishment, (according to Jer. xx. 7,) ἀπάτη, that is "a deceit," though it is beneficial in its results, and is brought about by God Himself as a pedagogical artifice "For many wise men, or such as were thought wise, having apprehended the truth, and rejected the delusion, respecting the divine punishments, gave themselves up to a vicious life, while it would have been much better for them to believe as they once did in the undying worm and the fire which is not quenched."

It is, I believe, owing to this principle of reserve in communicating certain points of religious knowledge, that we find comparatively so little on the subject of Restitution in the public writings of the early Fathers. For, in accordance with the Apostle's words, "Which things we *speak*," and again, "We *speak* wisdom among them that are perfect," (1 Cor. ii. 6, 13,) they felt that they might "speak" to mature and well-instructed souls things which it would not be wise to "write" for all.

But to pass on to a second witness to the doctrine of Restitution. Clement of Alexandria, who, in the 5th and 6th books of his *Stromata* has written so fully on this subject of reserve,—see especially book 6, chapter 15,—in his notes on the Epistle of St. John, (*Adumbrat. in Ep.* i. *Johan.*, printed at the end of his Treatise, *Quis dives salvetur*, p. 1009, Potter's Edit.) has these words :—

"Nec solum autem, inquit, *pro nostris peccatis* Dominus propitiator est, hoc est fidelium, *sed etiam pro toto mundo.* Proinde universos quidem salvat, sed alios per supplicia convertens, alios autem spontaneâ assequentes voluntate, et cum honoris dignitate, *ut omne genu flectatur Ei, cœlestium, terrestrium, et infernorum*, hoc est, angeli, homines, et animæ, quæ ante adventum Ejus de hâc vitâ migravere temporali."

That is, "The Lord, he says, is a propitiation, 'not for our sins only,' that is, of the faithful, ' but also for the whole world.' Therefore He indeed saves all universally ; but some as converted by punishments, others by voluntary submission, thus obtaining the honour and dignity, that 'to Him every knee shall bow, of things in heaven, and things in earth, and things under the earth,' that is angels, and men, and souls who departed this life before His coming into the world."

Other writers of the Alexandrian School might be here cited as holding substantially the same doctrine.

The following passage from Theophilus of Antioch, A.D. 168, is perhaps even more striking ; (*Ad Autolychum*, lib. ii. c. 26 :)

Καὶ τοῦτο δὲ ὁ θεὸς μεγάλην εὐεργεσίαν παρέσχε τῷ ἀνθρώπῳ, τὸ μὴ διαμεῖναι αὐτὸν εἰς τὸν αἰῶνα ἐν ἁμαρτίᾳ ὄντα, ἀλλὰ τρόπῳ τινὶ ἐν ὁμοιώματι ἐξορισμοῦ ἐξέβαλεν αὐτὸν ἐκ τοῦ παραδείσου, ὅπως διὰ τῆς ἐπιτιμίας τακτῷ ἀποτίσας χρόνῳ τὴν ἁμαρτίαν καὶ παιδευθεὶς ἐξ ὑστέρου ἀνακληθῇ. Διὸ καὶ πλασθέντος ἀνθρώπου ἐν τῷ κόσμῳ τούτῳ, μυστηριωδῶς ἐν τῇ Γενέσει γέγραπται, ὡς δὶς αὐτοῦ ἐν τῷ παραδείσῳ τεθέντος· ἵνα τὸ μὲν ἅπαξ ᾖ πεπληρωμένον ὁτὲ ἐτέθη· τὸ δὲ δεύτερον μέλλῃ πληροῦσθαι μετὰ τὴν ἀνάστασιν καὶ κρίσιν. Οὐ μὴν ἀλλὰ καὶ καθάπερ σκεῦός τι, ἐπὰν πλασθὲν αἰτίαν τινὰ σχῇ, ἀναχωνεύεται, ἢ ἀναπλάσσεται, εἰς τὸ γενέσθαι καινὸν καὶ ὁλόκληρον· οὕτω γίνεται καὶ τῷ ἀνθρώπῳ διὰ θανάτου· δυνάμει γὰρ τέθραυσται, ἵνα ἐν τῇ ἀναστάσει ὑγιὴς εὑρεθῇ, λέγω δὲ ἄσπιλος, καὶ δίκαιος, καὶ ἀθάνατος.

That is, "And God shewed great kindness to man, in this, that He did not suffer him to continue being in sin for ever; but, as it were, by a kind of banishment, cast him out of Paradise, in order that, having by punishment expiated, within an appointed time, the sin, and having been disciplined, he should afterwards be recalled. Wherefore also, when man had been formed in this world, it is mystically written in Genesis, as if he had been twice placed in Paradise; so that the one was fulfilled when he was placed there, and the second will be fulfilled after the resurrection and judgment. Nay further, just as a vessel, when on being fashioned it has some flaw, is re-moulded or re-made, that it may become new and entire; so also it happens to man by death. For he is broken up by force, that in the resurrection he may be found whole, I mean spotless, and righteous, and immortal."

Irenæus, A.D. 182, holds the same view, of death being a merciful provision for a fallen creature. His words, (*Contr. Hær.* lib. iii. c. 23, § 6,) are:—

"Quapropter et ejecit eum de paradiso, et a ligno vitæ longè transtulit; non invidens ei lignum vitæ, quemadmodum quidam audent dicere, sed miserans ejus, ut non perseveraret semper transgressor, neque immortale esset quod esset circa eum peccatum, et malum interminabile et insanabile."

That is, "Wherefore also He drove him out of Paradise, and removed him far from the tree of life, not because He envied him the tree of life, as some dare to assert, but because He pitied him, [and desired] that he should not continue always a sinner, and that the sin which surrounded him should not be immortal, and the evil interminable and irremediable."

Origen has the same doctrine, (*Hom.* xviii. *in Jerem.*) as have others of the Fathers.

To the same effect is the whole work of Athenagoras, A.D. 177, *On the Resurrection.* The argument throughout is so connected that it is not easy to make a brief extract. The following concluding sentence of the work may however sufficiently shew the general doctrine: (*De Resurr.* c. xxv.)

Τούτου δ' ἐξ ἀνάγκης ἑπομένου, δεῖ πάντως γενέσθαι τῶν νεκρωθέντων ἢ καὶ πάντη διαλυθέντων σωμάτων ἀνάστασιν, καὶ

N

178   *The Restitution of All Things.*

τοὺς αὐτοὺς ἀνθρώπους συστῆναι πάλιν. . . . ταύτης γὰρ γενομένης
καὶ τὸ τῇ φύσει τῶν ἀνθρώπων πρόσφορον ἐπακολουθεῖ τέλος. Τέλος
δὲ ζωῆς ἐμφρονος καὶ λογικῆς κρίσεως οὐκ ἂν ἁμάρτοι τις εἰπὼν τὸ
τούτοις ἀπερισπάστως συνδιαιωνίζειν, οἷς μάλιστα καὶ πρώτως ὁ
φυσικὸς συνήρμοσται λόγος, τῇ τε θεωρίᾳ τοῦ ὄντος καὶ τῶν ἐκείνῳ
δεδογμένων ἀπαύστως ἐπαγάλλεσθαι· κἂν οἱ πολλοὶ τῶν ἀνθρώπων,
ἐμπαθέστερον καὶ σφοδρότερον τοῖς τῇδε προσπεπονθότες, ἄστοχοι
τούτου διατελῶσιν. Οὐ γὰρ ἀκυροῖ τὴν κοινὴν ἀποκλήρωσιν τὸ
πλῆθος τῶν ἀποπιπτόντων τοῦ προσήκοντος αὐτοῖς τέλους, ἰδια-
ζούσης τῆς ἐπὶ τούτοις ἐξετάσεως, καὶ τῆς ἑκάστῳ συμμετρουμένης
ὑπὲρ τῶν εὖ ἢ κακῶς βεβιωμένων τιμῆς ἢ δίκης.

That is, "And as this follows of necessity, there must by
all means be a resurrection of the bodies which are dead or
even entirely dissolved, and the same men must be formed
anew. . . . for if this takes place, the end befitting the nature
of men follows also. And the end of an intelligent life and of
a rational judgment, we shall make no mistake in saying, is
to be occupied uninterruptedly with those objects to which
the natural reason is chiefly and primarily adapted, and to
delight unceasingly in the contemplation of Him who is, and
of His decrees; notwithstanding that the majority of men,
because they are affected too passionately and too violently by
things below, pass through life without attaining this object.
For the large number of those who fail of the end that belongs
to them does not make void the common lot, since the examina-
tion relates to individuals, and the reward or punishment of
lives ill or well spent is proportioned to what each has done."

We find the same doctrine just hinted at in Gregory of
Nazianzus; (*Orat. Quadrag.* §. 36. p. 664, Ed. Paris. 1630.)

Οἶδα καὶ πῦρ οὐ καθαρτήριον, ἀλλὰ κολαστήριον, εἴτε Σοδομι-
τικὸν . . . . εἴτε τὸ ἡτοιμασμένον τῷ διαβόλῳ, ... εἴτε ὃ πρὸ
προσώπου Κυρίου πορεύεται, καὶ τούτων ἔτι φοβερώτερον, ὃ τῷ
ἀκοιμήτῳ σκώληκι συντέτακται, μὴ σβεννύμενον, ἀλλὰ διαιωνίζον
τοῖς πονηροῖς. Πάντα γὰρ ταῦτα ἀφανιστικῆς ἐστι δυνάμεως· εἰ
μὴ τὸ φίλον κ'ανταῦθα νοεῖν τοῦτο φιλανθρωπότερον, καὶ τοῦ
κολάζοντος ἐπαξίως.

That is, "There is another fire, I know, not for purging,
but for punishing; whether it be of that kind by which Sodom

was destroyed, ... or whether that prepared for the devil,
. . . . or that which goes before the face of the Lord, and
which, more to be dreaded than all, is conjoined with the undying worm, which is not quenched, but lasts perpetually, (or
through the ages) for the wicked. All these are of a destructive
nature. Unless even here to regard this as done in love is
more in accordance with (God's) love to man, and more worthy
of Him who punishes."

Gregory of Nyssa speaks more clearly ; (*Dial. de Animâ et
Resurrect.* tom. iii. p. 227, Ed. Paris. 1638.)

Χρὴ γὰρ πάντη καὶ πάντως ἐξαιρεθῆναι ποτὲ τὸ κακὸν ἐκ τοῦ
ὄντος· . . . . ἐπειδὴ γὰρ ἔξω τῆς προαιρέσεως. ἡ κακία εἶναι φύσιν
οὐκ ἔχει, ὅταν πᾶσα προαίρεσις ἐν τῷ θεῷ γένηται, εἰς παντελῆ
ἀφανισμὸν ἡ κακία μὴ χωρήσει, τῷ μηδὲν αὐτῆς ἀπολειφθῆναι
δοχεῖον ; κ. τ. λ.

And again, (*Catechet. Orat.* cap. 26, tom. iii. p. 85,) Christ
is spoken of as τόν τε ἄνθρωπον τῆς κακίας ἐλευθερῶν, καὶ αὐτὸν
τῆς κακίας εὑρετὴν ἰώμενος.

That is,—" For it is needful that evil should some day be
wholly and absolutely removed out of the circle of being.
. . . . For inasmuch as it is not in the nature of evil to exist
without the will, when every will comes to be in God, will
not evil go on to absolute extinction, by reason of there being
no receptacle of it left."

And again, in his *Catechetical Orations,* (chapter 26,)
Christ is spoken of as " the One who both delivers man from
evil, and who heals the inventor of evil himself."

Both the passages, and their contexts, are well worth
turning to. Referring to them Neander says, (*Church Hist.*
vol. iv. p. 455,) " We may notice here another after-influence
of the great Origen upon individual church-teachers, . . .
as for example on Didymus, and Gregory Nazianzen. Though
in the writings of Didymus, which have come to our knowledge,
there are no distinct traces to be found of the doctrine of
Restoration, (ἀποκατάστασις,) yet in his work *De Trinitate,*
published by Mingarelli, (Bologna 1769.) an intimation of
this kind may be found in his exposition and application of the
passage in Philipp. ii. 10, where, in reference to the καταχθόνια

as well as the ἐπίγεια, he speaks of 'every knee bowing at the name of Jesus:' (lib. iii. c. 10.) But this particular doctrine was expounded and maintained with the greatest ability in works written expressly for that purpose by Gregory of Nyssa. God, he maintained, had created rational beings in order that they might be self-conscious and free vessels for the communications of the original fountain of all good. All punishments are means of purification, ordained by divine love to purge rational beings from moral evil, and to restore them back to that communion with God which corresponds to their nature. God would not have permitted the existence of evil, unless He had foreseen that by the Redemption all rational beings would in the end, according to their destination, attain to the same blessed fellowship with Himself."

Now when it is borne in mind that Gregory of Nazianzus presided at the Second General Council, and that to Gregory of Nyssa tradition ascribes all those additions to the original Nicene Creed, which were made at the same Second General Council, and which we now recite as portions of it, (Nicephor. *Eccl. Hist.* lib. xii. c. 13,)—when we remember the esteem in which the name and works of this same Gregory of Nyssa have ever been held, both during his life and since his death, and that he was referred to both by the Fifth and Seventh General Councils, as amongst the highest authorities of the Church, (Tillemont, *Mémoires*, tom. ix. p. 601,)—we shall be better able to judge the worth of the assertion, which is sometimes made, that the doctrine of final restitution is a heresy.

Diodorus of Tarsus, the tutor of Chrysostom, in his work on the Incarnation, (*De Œconomiâ*,) may also be cited as holding the same view; as also Theodore of Mopsuestia, the most distinguished critic of the Syrian School; (*Comment. in Evang.*) The passages are given in Assemanni *Biblioth. Orient.* tom. iii. part. i. pp. 323, 324.

Here perhaps I ought to add, that, while the doctrine of Universal Restoration was clearly held by the above-named Fathers, two even earlier Christian writers, Justin Martyr and Irenæus, seem to have held the doctrine of the annihilation of the wicked. Justin Martyr, in his *First Apology*, c. viii., says

indeed that the wicked will undergo "everlasting punishment;"
but elsewhere, (in *Dial. c. Tryph.* c. 5,) he plainly says, that
"those who have appeared worthy of God die no more, but
others are punished as long as God wills them to exist and be
punished "—*ἐστ' ἂν αὐτὰς καὶ εἶναι καὶ κολάζεσθαι ὁ θεὸς θέλῃ.*
Irenæus has the same language. "The Father of all," he
says, "imparts continuance for ever and ever to those who
are saved; for life does not arise from us, nor from our own
nature, but is bestowed according to the grace of God. He
therefore who shall keep the life given to him, and render
thanks to Him who imparted it, shall receive also length of
days for ever and ever. But he who shall reject it, and shew
himself ungrateful to his Maker, deprives himself of continuance
for ever and ever"—ipse se privat in sæculum sæculi perse-
verantiâ. (*Contr. Hæres.* lib. ii. c. 34, § 3.) We find the same
doctrine also in the Clementine Homilies, (*Hom.* iii. 6.)

It is instructive also to notice how Augustine, the great
champion of the doctrine of endless punishment, writes of
those who held Universal Restoration. He says, (*De Civ. Dei*,
lib. xxi. c. 17.)—

"Nunc jam cum misericordibus nostris agendum esse video
et pacificè disputandum, qui vel omnibus illis hominibus quos
justissimus Judex dignos gehennæ supplicio judicabit, vel qui-
busdam eorum, nolunt credere pœnam sempiternam futuram,
sed post certi temporis metam pro cujusque peccati quantitate
longioris sive brevioris eos inde existimant liberandos."

That is—"And now I see I must have a gentle disputation
with certain tender hearts of our own religion, who are unwilling to believe that everlasting punishment will be inflicted,
either on all those whom the just Judge shall condemn to the
pains of hell, or even on some of them, but who think that after
certain periods of time, longer or shorter according to the proportion of their crimes, they shall be delivered out of that state."

Augustine's "gentle disputation," thus introduced, occupies
several succeeding chapters of the same book. In chapter 18 he
alludes to some of the passages, such as Psalm lxxvii. 7-9, on
which these "tender hearts" rested their hopes, and to the
view, then held by some, (see chapters 18, 24, and 27,) that

the saints would be the instruments for saving all. His main reply, in chapter 23, is that the punishment of the wicked, according to S. Matt. xxv. 46, is as everlasting as the kingdom prepared for the righteous. The passage is worth turning to. To me one chief point of interest in it lies in the evidence it affords, that the views which Augustine combats were in his day held, and could be defended, by true Catholics, " nostri misericordes," even in the West, and that Augustine only proposes "gently to dispute," " pacificè disputandum," with them. I may add that in another place also, (*Enchirid. ad Laurent.* c. 29,) Augustine refers to the " very many " (imo quam plurimi,) in his day, " who, though not denying the Holy Scriptures, do not believe in endless torments."

Even Jerome, at the end of his *Commentary on Isaiah*, (lib. xviii. in cap. lxvi.) could write :—

" Porro qui volunt supplicia aliquando finiri, et licet post multa tempora tamen terminum habere tormenta, his utuntur testimoniis : *Quum intraverit plenitudo gentium, tunc omnis Israel salvus fiet.* Et iterum : *Conclusit Deus omnia sub peccato, ut omnibus misereatur.* Et rursum : *Benedicam te, Domine, quoniam iratus es mihi. Avertisti faciem a me, et misertus es mei.* Dominus quoque loquitur ad peccatorem : *Quum ira furoris fuerit, rursus sanabo.* Et hoc est quod in alio loco dicitur : *Quàm grandis multitudo bonitatis tuæ, Domine, quam abscondisti timentibus te.* Quæ omnia replicant, asseverare cupientes, post cruciatus atque tormenta, futura refrigeria : quæ nunc abscondenda sunt ab his quibus timor utilis est, ut, dum supplicia reformidant, peccare desistant. Quod nos Dei solius debemus scientiæ derelinquere, cujus non solum misericordiæ sed et tormenta in pondere sunt, et novit quem, quomodo, et quamdiu, debet judicare. Solumque dicamus, quod humanæ convenit fragilitati : *Domine, ne in furore tuo arguas me, neque in irâ tuâ corripias me.*"

That is,—" But further, those who maintain that punishment will one day come to an end, and that torments have a limit, though after long periods, use as proofs the following testimonies of Scripture :—' When the fulness of the Gentiles shall have come in, then all Israel shall be saved ; ' and again,

'God hath concluded all in unbelief, that He might have mercy upon all;' and again, ' I will praise Thee, O Lord, for Thou wast angry with me; Thou hadst turned thy face from me; but Thou hast comforted me.' The Lord Himself also says to the sinner, 'When the fierceness of my wrath hath passed, I will heal him.' And this is what is said in another place:—'Oh, how great is thy goodness, which Thou hast laid up for them that fear Thee.' All which testimonies of Scripture they urge in reply against us, while they earnestly assert that after certain sufferings and torments there will be restoration. All which nevertheless they allow should not now be openly told to those with whom fear yet acts as a motive, and who may be kept from sinning by the terror of punishment. But this question we ought to leave to the wisdom of God alone, whose judgments as well as mercies are by weight and measure, and who well knows whom, and how, and how long, He ought to judge."

To these testimonies I add one more from Facundus, bishop of Hermiane, who was chosen by the bishops of Africa to represent them at Constantinople in their protest against an edict of Justinian's, which seemed to them to impugn the judgment of the Council of Chalcedon; and of whose writings Neander says, (*Church Hist.* vol. iv. p. 274,) that they are "eminently characterized by qualities seldom to be met with in this age,—a freedom of spirit unshackled by human fear, and a candid, thorough criticism, superior in many respects to the prejudices of the times." The passage is interesting too, as shewing that when Facundus wrote, other bishops besides himself regarded those who held the doctrine of the final salvation of all men to be "most holy and glorious teachers." Facundus (*Pro defens. trium capit.* lib. iv. c. 4; in Sirmondi's *Opera Varia*, tom. 2. p. 384. Ed. Venet. 1728,) says,—

"His omnibus accedit et confessio Domitiani Galatæ Ancyrencis olim episcopi. . . . Nam in libello quem ad Vigilium scripsit, conquerens de his qui contradicebant dogmatibus Origenis, asserentis animas humanas ante corpora in quâdam beatâ vitâ præextitisse, et omnes quæ fuerint æterno supplicio destinatæ in pristinam beatitudinem, cum diabolo et angelis ejus, restitui; dicit etiam hæc: ' Prosiluerunt ad anathematizandos sanctissimos et gloriosissimos doctores, sub occasione eorum quæ de præexistentiâ et restitutione mota sunt dogmatum; sub specie quidem OrigeLis, omnes autem qui ante eum et post eum fuerant sanctos anathematizantes.' "

' That is,—" To all this is also to be added the confession of Domitian of Galatia, formerly bishop of Ancyra. . . . For in the book which he wrote to Vigilius, where he is complaining of those who contradicted tHe doctrines of Origen,—who maintained that the souls of men had pre-existed in some state of blessedness before they caffe into bodies, and that all those who were doomed to the eternal punishment should, together with the devil and his angels, be restored to their former state of blessedness,—he says, ' They have hastily run out to anathematize most holy and glorious teachers on account of those doctrines which have been advanced concerning pre-existence and restitution; and this indeed under pretext of Origen, but thereby anathematizing all those saints who were before and have been after him.' "

These passages shew how widely the doctrine of Universal Restoration was held in the Church during the Second, Third, Fourth, and Fifth Centuries. I will now give two or three extracts, which might easily be multiplied, as evidencing the views of many of the Fathers, not only as to God's end in punishment, and the purification of all by fire, but also as to the ministry of Christ and His elect after death to the departed.

First, as to God's end in punishment.—Clement of Alexandria (*Strom.* lib. vii. cap. 16,) says,—Κολάζει πρὸς τὸ χρήσιμον καὶ κοινῇ καὶ ἰδίᾳ τοῖς κολαζομίνοις: that is, "He punishes for their good those who are punished, whether collectively or individually." Clement continually repeats the same doctrine: see *Strom.* lib. i. cap. 27; lib. vii. cap. 2, and cap. 6; *Pædag.* lib. i. cap. 8.

So too Theodoret (*Hom. in Ezech.* cap. vi. vers. 6,) says,— 'Εδειξε τῆς τιμωρίας τὰς αἰτίας· ἰατρικῶς γὰρ ὁ φιλάνθρωπος κολάζει Δεσπότης ἵνα παύσῃ τῆς ἀσεβείας τὸν δρόμον· ταῦτα γὰρ πάντα, φησί, ποιῶ, καὶ τὴν ἐρημίαν ἐπάξω, ἵνα σβέσω τὴν περὶ τὰ εἴδωλα μανίαν καὶ λύτταν. That is, "He shews here the reason for punishment; for the Lord, the lover of men, torments us only to cure us, that He may put a stop to the course of our iniquity. All these things, He says, I do, and bring in desolation, that I may extinguish men's madness and rage after idols."

Then as to the baptism by fire,—Gregory of Nazianzus, in a passage where he is alluding to the Novatians, (*Orat.* xxxix. § 19, p. 690. Ed. Paris. 1778,) says,—Οὗτοι μὲν οὖν, εἰ μὲν βούλοιντο, τὴν ἡμετέραν ὁδὸν καὶ Χριστοῦ, εἰ δὲ μὴ, τὴν ἑαυτῶν πορευέσθωσαν· τυχὸν ἐκεῖ τῷ πυρὶ βαπτισθήσονται τῷ τελευταίῳ βαπτίσματι, τῷ ἐπιπονωτέρῳ καὶ μακροτέρῳ, ὃ ἐσθίει ὡς χόρτον τὴν ὕλην, καὶ ἁαπανᾷ πάσης κακίας κουφότητα. That is, "These, if they will, may go our way, which indeed is Christ's; but if not, let them go their own way. In another place perhaps they shall be baptized with fire, that last baptism, which is not only very painful, but enduring also; which eats up, as if it were hay, all defiled matter, and consumes all vanity and vice."

So too Gregory of Nyssa (*Orat. pro Mortuis*, ad. fin. p. 634, Ed. Paris. 1638,) says,—Ὡς ἂν οὖν καὶ ἡ ἐξουσία μένοι τῇ φύσει, καὶ τὸ κακὸν ἀπογένοιτο, ταύτην εὗρεν ἡ σοφία τοῦ Θεοῦ τὴν ἐπίνοιαν, τὸ ἐᾶσαι τὸν ἄνθρωπον ἐν οἷς ἐβουλήθη γενέσθαι, ἵνα γευσάμενος τῶν κακῶν ὧν ἐπεθύμησει, καὶ τῇ πείρᾳ μαθὼν οἷα ἀνθ' οἵων ἠλλάξετο, παλινδρομήσῃ διὰ τῆς ἐπιθυμίας ἑκουσίως πρὸς τὴν πρώτην μακαριότητα. . . . ἤτοι κατὰ τὴν παροῦσαν ζωὴν διὰ προσευχῆς καὶ φιλοσοφίας ἐκκαθαρθεὶς, ἢ μετὰ τὴν ἐνθένδε μετανά-στασιν διὰ τῆς τοῦ καθαρσίου πυρὸς χωνείας. That is,—"Wherefore that at the same time liberty of free-will should be left to nature and yet the evil be purged away, the wisdom of God discovered this plan, to suffer man to do what he would, that having tasted the evil which he desired, and learning by experience for what wretchedness he had bartered away the blessings he had, he might of his own will hasten back with desire to the first blessedness, . . . either being purged in this life through prayer and discipline, or after his departure hence through the furnace of cleansing fire."

So too Ambrose, (*Serm.* xx. § 12, *in Psalm.* cxviii. p. 1225, Ed. Paris. 1686.)—"Omnes oportet per ignem probari, quicunque ad Paradisum redire desiderant; non enim otiosè, scriptum est, quòd, ejectis Adam et Evâ de Paradisi sede, posuit Deus in

exitu Paradisi gladium igneum versatilem. Omnes oportet
transire per flammas, sive ille Johannes Evangelista sit, quem
ita dilexit Dominus, ... sive ille sit Petrus qui claves ac-
cepit regni cœlorum, &c." That is,—"It is necessary that all
should be proved by fire, whosoever they are that desire to return to Paradise. For not in vain is it written, that, when
Adam and Eve were expelled from Paradise, God placed at the
outlet a flaming sword which turned every way. All therefore
must pass through these fires, whether it be that Evangelist
John whom the Lord so loved, ... or Peter, who received
the keys of the kingdom of heaven, &c."

So again, (*in Psalm.* i. § 54, p. 763, Ed. Paris. 1686,) he
says,—"Salvator duo genera resurrectionis posuit, ut Johannes
in Apocalypsi dixit, *Beatus qui habet partem in primâ resurrec-
tione*; isti enim sine judicio veniunt ad gratiam. Qui autem
non veniunt ad primam resurrectionem, sed ad secundam
reservantur, isti urentur donec impleant tempora inter primam
et secundam resurrectionem: aut si non impleverint, diutius
in supplicio permanebunt." That is,—"Our Saviour has appointed two kinds of resurrection, in accordance with which
John says, in the Apocalypse, 'Blessed is he that hath part in
the first resurrection'; for such come to grace without the
judgment. As for those who do not come to the first, but are
reserved until the second, resurrection, these shall be burnt,
until they fulfil their appointed times, between the first and
the second resurrection; or, if they should not have fulfilled
them then, they shall remain still longer in punishment."

The same views are constantly stated by Origen; (*Hom.*
vi. § 4, *in Exod.; Hom.* xxv. § 6, *in Num.; Hom.* iii. § 1,
in Psalm. xxxvi. 14; and elsewhere;) and in more general
terms by Clement of Alexandria; (*Strom.* lib. vii. c. 6.)

As to the ministry of Christ and His elect after death to
the departed, several of the Fathers speak very distinctly.

Clement of Alexandria (*Strom.* lib. vi. cap. 6, p. 763, Ed.
Potter,) says,—διόπερ ὁ Κύριος εὐηγγελίσατο καὶ τοῖς ἐν ᾅδου,
κ. τ. λ. Further on, in the same chapter, he says, Καὶ οἱ
ἀπόστολοι καθάπερ ἐνταῦθα, οὕτως κ'ἀκεῖ (in hades) τοὺς ἐξ ἐθνῶν
ἐπιτηδείους εἰς ἐπιστροφὴν εὐηγγελίσαντο, κ. τ. λ. That is,

" Wherefore the Lord preached the gospel to them also who were in hades, &c. . . . And His apostles also, as here, so there also, preached the gospel to those of the heathen who were ready to be converted." After which immediately follows a quotation from the *Shepherd* of Hermas, (lib. iii. cap. 16.) to the same effect.

We have the same doctrine stated again by Clement, in the second book of the *Stromata*, and the ninth chapter ; (p. 452, Ed. Potter;) also by Ignatius ; (*Epist. ad Trall.* cap. ix.) and by Irenæus ; (*Hær.* lib. iv. cap. 22.) and by Justin Martyr; (*Dial. c. Tryph.* cap. 72.)

The following passage from Gieseler, (*Eccl. Hist.* vol. i. § 82,) will shew that these views have not been confined to followers of Origen. He says,—"The opinion of the indestructible capacity for reformation in all rational creatures, and the finiteness of the torments of hell, was so common even in the West, and so widely diffused among opponents of Origen, that though it might not have sprung up without the influence of his school, yet it had become quite independent of it."

My own conviction, the result of some acquaintance with the Fathers, is, that the doctrine of Universal Restitution was held by many who in their public teaching distinctly asserted endless punishment. To take the great and good Chrysostom as an example. If we only looked at his statements as to the end of punishment, we should say that he must also hold Universal Restoration. For his doctrine is, that "if punishment were an evil to the sinner, God would not have added evils to the evil ; " that " all punishment is owing to His loving us, by pains to recover us and lead us to Him, and to deliver us from sin which is worse than hell." (*Hom.* ix. *in Ep. ad Rom.* v. 11. See also *Hom.* v. § 13, *de Statuis*, and *Hom.* iii. § 2, *in Ep. ad Philem.* i. 25.) Yet in his sermons he repeatedly states the doctrine of everlasting punishment; (e.g. *Hom.* ix. § 1, 2, *in Ep.* 1. *ad Cor.* iii. 12; *Hom.* x. § 6, *in Ep.* 2. *ad Cor.* v. 10; and *Hom.* viii. § 2, *in Ep.* 1. *ad Thess.* iv. 15; &c.) His view however of what he calls an " œconomy," (that is some particular line of conduct, whether of God or man, pursued for the benefit of certain other persons,) that

" those who are to derive benefit from an œconomy should be unacquainted with the course of it: otherwise the benefit of it will be lost; " (*Comment. in Galat.* ii. 5, 6;) and the strong feeling which he often expresses as to the evil of communicating certain higher truths to the uninitiated; (e.g. *Hom.* xl. § 2, *in Ep.* 1. *ad Cor.* xv. 29; and *Hom.* xviii. § 3, *in Ep.* 2. *ad Cor.* viii. 24;) go far to explain why in sermons addressed to the multitude he has spoken as he has on this subject. We know however, that, spite of his popular language as to everlasting punishment, among the accusations brought against him when he was summoned to the Synod of the Oak, one distinct charge was his Origenism. It is certainly significant, that, in his 39th Homily on the 1st Epistle to the Corinthians, he alludes to the opinion of those who asserted that St. Paul, in 1 Cor. xv. 28, taught an *ἀναίρεσις τῆς κακίας*, without answering it.

So again with Ambrose. Not only are there passages, in his book *De Bono Mortis*, which, as it appears to me, can never be reconciled with the doctrine of never-ending punishment, but the whole drift of the book is in an entirely opposite direction. For he asserts that "death is the end of sin;" (cap. iv.) that, even with the wicked, " it is worse to live to sin than to die in sin; for, while the wicked man lives, he encreases his sin: if he dies, he ceases to sin." (cap. vii.) The whole 4th chapter is to prove, that "death is altogether good, as well because it is the end of sin, as because it redeemed the world." In a word, according to Ambrose, sin is the great evil, while what we call death is God's means to deliver man from the evil; "for those who are unbelievers descend into hell, even while they live: though they seem to live with us, they are in hell." (cap. xii.) But all this is directly opposed to the popular notion of future punishment, which regards the second death as hopeless, endless torment.

A thoughtful reader too cannot but be struck with the way in which in their controversies with the Manichees and others, who held the eternity of two opposing principles of good and evil, the advocates of the truth, that there is but One God, only prove their point either by asserting that all evil shall one

day cease, or else by arguing that evil is really nothing. Thus
in the *Debate between Manes and Archelaus,* (A.D. 277,) the
truth that there is but One God, and He a good one, is only
sustained against the Manichean view by the declaration that
all evil may and will cease. "When," asks Manes, (§ 17,)
"will that happen which you tell of?" "I am only a man,"
replies Archelaus, "and do not know what will come: nevertheless I will not leave that point without saying something
on it." He afterwards says, (§ 29,) "Therefore it (death) has
an end, because it began in time; and that is true which was
spoken, 'Death is swallowed up in victory.' It is plain therefore that death cannot be unbegotten, seeing that it is shewn
to have both a beginning and an end." (Routh's *Reliq. Sacr.*
vol. v. p. 111. Ed. Oxon. 1848.) The argument of Athanasius
is, that evil in its own nature is nothing. "Those things,"
he says, "are, which are good: those things are not, which
are evil. And good things have being, because their patterns
are in God, who truly is; but evil things have not being,
because, nothing in themselves, they are the fictions of men."
And again, "As a substance, and in its own nature, evil is
nothing; the Creator has made all things." (*Orat c. Gentes,* c.
4, & 6. Opp. tom. i. pp. 4, 6.) Basil has the same doctrine:—
"Evil is no real thing, but a negation or privation." (*Hom.
Quod Deus non est auctor malorum,* c. 5.) Gregory of Nyssa
also uses very similar language. (*Orat. Catech.* c. 28.) And
so too Augustine, replying to the Manichees, says, "Who is
so blind as not to see that evil is that which is opposed to the
nature of a thing? And by this principle is your heresy re-
futed; for evil, as opposed to nature, is not a nature. But you
say that evil is a certain nature and substance. Then what is
opposed to nature struggles against it and would destroy it.
So that which exists tends to make non-existence. For nature
itself is only what is understood, after its kind, to be something. . . . If then you will consider the matter, evil consists
in this very thing, namely in a defection from being, and a ten-
dency to non-being." (*De Moribus Manich.* lib. ii. § 2, & 3.)
We find the same doctrine also in his *Confessions*: (lib. vii. c. 12.)
But if this be so, what becomes of Augustine's doctrine of

never-ending punishment, which surely is never-ending existence in evil?

So much then as to the views of some of the greatest
teachers of the Early Church. After Augustine's time, partly
through his great authority, but even more in consequence of
the general ignorance both of Greek and Hebrew, which for
centuries prevailed in the Western Church, and which kept
men from reading the Scriptures in the original languages, the
doctrine of Universal Restoration was well-nigh silenced in the
West until the revival of learning in the 16th century. My
own impression is that the doctrine of Purgatory, properly so
called, which gradually grew up from the 5th to the 7th century, in contradistinction to the earlier view of purifying fire
held by Clement of Alexandria and Origen, was a natural
result of the efforts of Augustine and others to silence the
doctrine of Restitution. In the 9th century, however, John
Scotus Erigena once again, and in the most decided way, bore
witness to the hope of Universal Restitution. Having at an
early age visited Greece, he brought back with him into the
West a system of doctrine which was the fruit of a careful
study of the Greek Fathers, particularly of Origen, Gregory of
Nyssa, and Maximus. For a brief but good account of this
writer's teaching, I may refer the reader to Oxenham's *Catholic
Doctrine of the Atonement*, Second Edition, pp. 151-154, or to
Neander's *Church History*, vol. vi. pp. 254-260. Since the Re-
formation many of our English divines,—among the Puritans,
Jeremiah White and Peter Sterry,—and in the English Church,
Richard Clarke, William Law, and George Stonehouse,—in
Scotland, Thomas Erskine of Linlathen and Bishop Ewing,—
and among those on the Continent, Bengel, Oberlin, Hahn, and
Tholuck,—have been believers in final restitution.

I may perhaps add here that it is confessed by the highest
authorities of the Roman Church, that the opinion of the miti-
gation or intermission of the sufferings of the damned, which
has been held by some, is nowhere condemned by the Catholic
Church. Dr. Newman in his *Grammar of Assent*, p. 417, has
quoted, without contradiction, and apparently with sympathy,

the following passage from Petavius, (*De Angelis,* ad. fin.)—
" De hâc damnatorum saltem hominum respiratione, *nihil adhuc certi decretum est ab Ecclesiâ Catholicâ; ut propterea non temerè tanquam absurda sit explodenda sanctissimorum Patrum hæc opinio;* quamvis a communi sensu Catholicorum hoc tempore sit aliena."

It ought not to be forgotten also, that our English Church, having in her original Forty-two Articles had a Forty-first, declaring of " Millenarians," that they " cast themselves head-long into a Jewish dotage," and a Forty-second, asserting, that " All men shall not be saved at length," within a very few years, in Elizabeth's reign, struck out both these Articles. Surely this is not without its significance. The Creeds, which are received both by East and West, not only make no mention whatever of endless punishment, but in their declaration of " the forgiveness of sins " seem to teach a very different doctrine.

Note C.
On Hebrews ii. 9, 16.

The possibility of the recovery of fallen angels is said to be absolutely negatived by the Apostle's words, in Hebrews ii. 16, that our Lord " took not on Him the nature of angels." Angels therefore, it is argued, cannot be restored.

But is it true that our Lord has never taken the nature of angels ? What then is taught in such Scriptures as Gen. xxii. 15, 16; xlviii. 16; Judges vi. 12, 14, 22, 23; xiii. 21, 22; Isa. lxiii. 9; Zech. iii. 1; Mal. iii. 1; Acts vii. 38; Col. ii. 10; &c.; where our Lord is shewn to have appeared before His Incarnation as an angel ?

In the next place, is it true that the verse in question really says that our Lord " took not on Him the nature of angels ? "   To answer this we have only to turn to the Original, where (as the marginal note of our Authorized Version shews even to an English reader,) the words, *οὐ γὰρ ἐπιλαμβάνεται,* translated in the Authorized Version *"took not on Him*

the nature of," are seen to be simply, "*is not laying hold of*";
the statement being, that Christ is not now laying hold of
angels, but only of the seed of Abraham.

That this is the meaning of ἐπιλαμβάνεται may be shewn
from countless passages, such for example as S. Matt. xiv. 31;
S. Luke ix. 47; Acts xvi. 19; xxiii. 19; Heb. viii. 9. See
also the LXX. in Gen. xxv. 26; Exod. iv. 4; and Judges xvi.
3, 21, &c. This verse therefore gives no support whatever to
the doctrine based on the translation (corrected in the margin)
of our Authorized English Version.

There is however a passage in the same second chapter of
the Epistle to the Hebrews, which, if we take what appears to
have been the original reading, teaches, as Bengel and others
have shewn, a very different doctrine. I allude to the 8th and
9th verses, where our Version reads, " that He *by the grace of
God* should taste death for every man." It is not generally
known that an older reading is, " that He should taste death for
all *excepting God*"; χωρὶς θεοῦ instead of χάριτι θεοῦ. This is
the way Ambrose, A.D. 370, quotes the verse; and long before
his time, when Origen wrote, A.D. 203, this was the usual
reading, though in his Commentary on S. John (tom. i. § 40,)
he allows that "in some copies," (ἐν τισι ἀντιγράφοις,) the other
reading was also then to be met with. The ancient Syriac
Version too has followed the reading χωρὶς θεοῦ. The following notes on the passage, from Cornelius a Lapide,—who
gives us Ambrose's exposition,—from Origen, and lastly from
Bengel, shew how strong the evidence is in favour of χωρὶς θεοῦ.

Cornelius a Lapide's note is as follows:—"Nota. Pro χάριτι,
id est, *gratiâ Dei*, Theodoretus, Theophylactus, et Œcume-
nius legunt χωρὶς θεοῦ, id est, *sine Deo*, vel *excepto Deo*, addunt-
que, ita corruptum esse hunc locum à Nestorianis; hinc enim
illi probant in Christo duas fuisse personas, et Deum ab
homine fuisse separatum. Verum ante Nestorium Ambrosius,
(*lib. de fide*, cap. 4,) legit quoque τὸ *sine Deo*; sicque
explicat: 'Christus pro omnibus sine Deo, id est, *excepto Deo*,
mortem gustavit, q.d. Christus pro omnibus, etiam angelis,
non autem pro Deo ipso, (Deum enim excipio,) mortuus est.

Non quasi angelos redemerit Christus, sed quod angelos
hominibus reconciliarit, eorumque lætitiam et gloriam auxerit,
dum sedes eorum, ex quibus collapsi erant dæmones, per
homines restauravit et replevit.'" Which explanation of the
words shews that Ambrose accepted the reading, χωρὶς θεοῦ,
though he would draw another conclusion from it.

Origen constantly quotes the passage, with the reading
χωρὶς θεοῦ; e.g. *Comment. in Johan.* tom. i. § 40; (vol. iv. p. 41.
Ed. Delarue, Paris, 1733–59;) and again tom. xxviii. § 14;
(vol. iv. pp. 392, 393.) And again in his *Comment. in Epist.
ad. Rom.* lib. iii. § 8; (vol. iv. p. 513.) And again lib. v. § 7,
of the same; (p. 560.) In quoting the verse in his *Commentary
on the Epistle to the Romans,* (lib. v. § 7. pp. 559, 560,) he
says, "Requiritur sanè, si in solis hominibus superabundet
gratia, in quibus abundavit aliquando peccatum; et an in nullo
superabundet gratia, nisi in quo abundavit peccatum; an et in
aliquibus potest superabundare gratia, in quibus nunquam vel
abundaverit vel fuerit peccatum. Et si quis illud aspiciat
quod dicit Apostolus, quia *pacificavit Christus per sanguinem
suum non solum quæ in terris sunt, sed et quæ in cælis,* et illud,
Ut sine Deo pro omnibus gustaret mortem, putabit et ibi
similiter aliquem abundantiam fuisse peccati, ut nihilominus
etiam gratiæ superabundantia fieret."

Bengel too evidently prefers the reading χωρίς. Having
pointed out, (*Gnomon,* in loco,) how nearly identical the
teaching of verses 8 and 9 is with that of 1 Cor. xv. 17, where,
as he observes, "in treating of the same Psalm, the same
verse, and the same words, 'All things put under Him,' the
Apostle states, that the 'All' admits of one most evident and
proper exception, saying, 'It is evident that He is excepted
which did put all things under Him,'"—Bengel goes on to say,
that "the same exception is made in this passage, only here it
is as to those for whom He tasted death. 'For all, excepting
God.'" He then thus sums up in favour of the reading χωρὶς
θεοῦ:—"Nunc quæritur, utra lectio genuina est. Non ignoro,
χάριτι plausibilius esse, quam χωρίς. Et sine labore ullo a me
impetrarem, ut hoc missum facerem, et illud amplecterer.

o

Sed ubi de verbo Dei, ubi de unico Dei verbulo agitur, nil temporis causâ statuere debemus. Facilius χωρὶς in χάριτι, quàm χάριτι in χωρὶς librariorum sedulitas, planiora omnia quærens, mutavit: et tamen χωρὶς remanet in monumentis antiquis, multis, gravibus. Neque lectionem hanc, neque interpretationem hic à nobis propositam, quisquam, ut spero, exagitabit: lectori tamen integrum est, rem amplius expendere."

LONDON : PRINTED BY
SPOTTISWOODE AND CO., NEW-STREET SQUARE
AND PARLIAMENT STREET

CPSIA information can be obtained at www.ICGtesting.com
Printed in the USA
LVOW010857170313

324629LV00014B/345/A

9 780559 949821